FOLENS

# Citizenship and PSHE

## BOOK TWO

### Eileen Osborne & Steph Yates

# To the reader

### What's this book about?
You might find that question hard to answer just by looking at the chapter headings. After all, what has Learning to relax got to do with Forms of government? The answer is YOU. This book is about you. It's about you as an individual, you as part of a family, you as part of the communities to which you belong and you as an active citizen in the twenty-first century. It's also about the people around you and about the United Kingdom as a whole. That's quite a lot to fit into one book.

### What can this book teach me?
There are probably plenty of facts and figures in this book that you don't yet know. For example, do you know the population of the UK or where the law stands on young people in employment? But this book is not really about facts and figures – it's more about forming your own opinions and learning to understand people and how they work, play and live together. To get the most out of it, you need to think about the topics, listen to other people's views, and be prepared to discuss your own ideas. If you let it, this book can help you to get on with yourself and other people better – and that's quite a lot to achieve.

### How will I use the book?
Your teacher will guide you through the lessons. Sometimes you will be writing and this could be notes, diagrams, stories, letters, plays or other types of writing. Sometimes you will be talking, either sharing your ideas, making plans or working in role as another character. You will also have chances to find out more by carrying out research and this may involve looking through books, newspapers or using the Internet. That's quite a lot of activities.

### Why are these lessons important?
These lessons are important because **you** are important, and the people around you are important. Anything that helps us understand each other and live together peacefully is important. That's quite enough for now.

EILEEN OSBORNE

STEPH YATES

# Contents

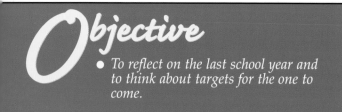

## Objective

- To reflect on the last school year and to think about targets for the one to come.

# A new school year

1. Make a list of the school subjects you studied last year. Copy the chart shown below. Now write down each of the subjects from your list in the column that shows how you feel you did in that subject.

| Did well | Did OK | Didn't do very well |
|---|---|---|
|  |  |  |

2. Look at your 'did well' column. If it is empty, think of some individual lessons where you did well. Now think about the subjects or lessons in this column. Write down some reasons suggesting why you did well in them.

**CONSIDER**

3. The list below shows one pupil's ideas of things that might help him do better next year. Which ones are things that are out of his control? Which ones are too vague to be helpful? Which ones could he really do that would make a difference?

> How I could do better next year
>
> Set aside time to do homework.
> Work harder.
> Have a teacher I like.
> Listen more.
> Get better at spelling.
> Read work to check for mistakes.
> Ask if I don't understand something.
> Learn my times tables.
> Get more sleep.
> Try to answer questions in class.
> Think more.

**FACT TO THINK ABOUT ... FACT TO THINK ABOUT ... FACT TO THINK ABOUT ...**

When a group of 13-year-olds was asked about their long-term targets, 75 per cent said 'to win the lottery'.

**KEY WORDS** | targets  responsibility  mature  short-term  long-term

4. Look back at your chart. For each subject in the 'did OK' and 'didn't do very well' columns, suggest at least one thing you could do to make sure you do better in that subject this year. Make sure they are suggestions that you could do that would make a real difference. Are there any things you could do that would help you in all your subjects?

5. Now choose two or three of your suggestions from question 4 that you are going to try. Write them out on a piece of paper or in your homework diary, where you can look at them from time to time.

6. The pupils below are talking about how they think their school year will be different from the last one. Read what they have to say, then write a paragraph saying how you think this year will be different from the last one.

**COMPARE**

> I will be treated more like an adult. I will be more responsible. I will be taking German.

> I will be in a different set for Maths. I will have more homework. I will have a new form tutor. The work will get harder. I will be expected to behave more maturely.

7. So far in this lesson, you have thought about last year, this year, things you will try to do and things that might be different. It's now time to think about your targets for the short- and long-term future. Divide your page into four and label the sections 'end of term', 'end of school year', 'when I leave school' and 'when I'm 25'. In each box, write down at least one thing that you hope to have achieved by then.

### Objective
- To focus on your strengths and begin thinking about possible career choices for the future.

# Future hopes

**BRAINSTORM**

**1.** As a class, use half the board to brainstorm strengths a person may have. You won't be able to list every strength there is but try to get a variety. The ideas below may help to get you thinking.

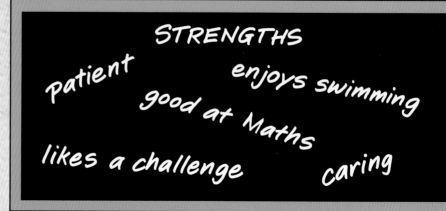

STRENGTHS

Patient

good at Maths

enjoys swimming

likes a challenge

caring

**2.** Now use the other side of the board to brainstorm weaknesses a person may have.

**3.** Working on your own, take a piece of paper and write down ten of your strengths and four weaknesses. Do not write your name on the piece of paper. Your teacher will give you a number to write instead.

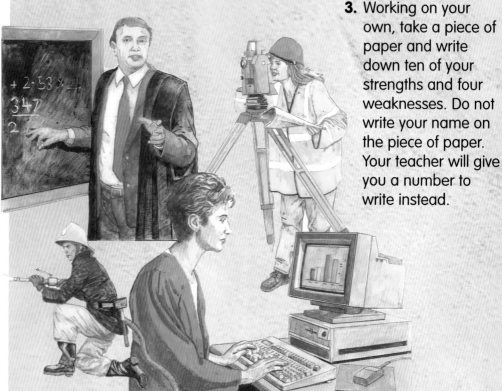

**FACT TO THINK ABOUT ... FACT TO THINK ABOUT ... FACT TO THINK ABOUT ...**

Experts predict that, on average, a person will retrain for different jobs at least three times during his or her working life.

| KEY WORDS | job   career   work   training   careers plan   careers officer |
| --- | --- |

**DISCUSS**

4. Your teacher will collect in the pieces of paper, then hand them out again so that everyone has someone else's list. Get together in groups of four or five. As a group, look at each of the lists you have. Think about the strengths and weaknesses and talk about jobs that might be suitable for a person with that profile. Write down three job suggestions on each sheet.

5. Return the lists to their original owners. What do you think about the job suggestions on your list? Say why you would or would not consider doing each one.

**RESEARCH**

6. Choose one job (which may or may not be on your list) and design a poster showing all the qualities and skills a person would need for that job. Find out what education and training someone would need for that job and include that on your poster too.

7. What new thoughts have you had about yourself and your career plans from this lesson?

**CONSIDER**

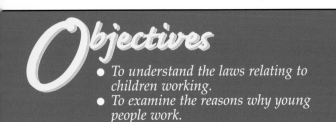

## Objectives

- To understand the laws relating to children working.
- To examine the reasons why young people work.

# A part-time job

**1.** Brainstorm jobs for which people of school age can get paid. Why do school children choose to work? Are there any disadvantages of working when you are still at school?

**2.** Read the newspaper report below.

# CHILD LABOUR LAWS NEED TIGHTENING

Up to half of children aged between 13 and 16 across the nation have part-time jobs, and as many as 750 000 of them are working illegally. Council officials in one area are now thinking of introducing new by-laws to regulate child labour. Suggestions include banning children under 15 from working on milk rounds, in amusement arcades, collecting money, or working in nightclubs and theatres. Children under 13 will also be barred from delivering newspapers, working in stables, hotels, shelf stacking and even washing cars.

Council child employment officer, Gary North, says that the situation at the moment is unworkable, with too many employers and children unaware of the laws. He said, "About 4000 children have part-time jobs in our area but only 676 are registered with the council. This makes it very difficult to monitor conditions. We recently investigated a case of a 12-year-old working in a burger bar. He shouldn't have been working at all, let alone in a kitchen. At the moment, all we can do is slap the employer's wrists. We don't have any real powers until the Government gives us some."

Estimates suggest that, nationally, only seven per cent of working children are registered. A recent Union report found that 44 per cent of working children had at least one job-related injury. It also claimed that unscrupulous bosses encouraged children to play truant by offering them work during school hours. Gary North commented that, "No one wants to stop children from working, within reason, but they have to be protected. Part-time work should be safe and it should never harm a child's school performance."

Children under the age of 16 may not be employed in a factory, although they may work in a small industrial firm if all the other workers are members of their family.

| **KEY WORDS** | legal   illegal   child labour |
| --- | --- |

**CONSIDER**

**3.** Why do you think the council wanted to ban children aged under 15 from working on milk rounds? Should a 12-year-old be working in a kitchen? Do you think they should be working at all? Does part-time work affect children's school performance?

**4.** The box below shows some of the laws relating to children working, but by-laws vary in different places so you may need to find out about the law in your area. Read the points below and talk about why they have been made into laws. Do you think they are a good idea?

### Children and the law

- No child under the age of 13 can be employed.
- Children between the ages of 13 and school leaving age may be employed part-time but not:
  - during school hours on any day when the school is open
  - before 7am or after 7pm on any day
  - for more than two hours on a school day or Sunday
  - in any job requiring lifting or moving heavy objects.

**5.** Design a leaflet for school pupils explaining the laws relating to children working in your area.

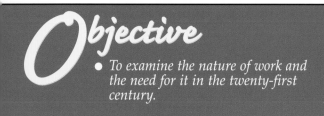

# The nature of work

**BRAINSTORM**

**1.** Brainstorm a list of reasons why people work. Which of these reasons would encourage you to work?

**CONSIDER**

**2.** The pictures below show people at work in the 1920s. How is each of these jobs done in the United Kingdom today? Which jobs today wouldn't have existed in the 1920s?

**FACT TO THINK ABOUT ... FACT TO THINK ABOUT ... FACT TO THINK ABOUT ...**

Some experts predict that, by 2050, pupils will be taught by a 'virtual reality' teacher.

| KEY WORDS | job satisfaction   work ethic   professional   manual worker   blue-collar worker   white-collar worker |
|---|---|

**3.** As well as types of work changing, working conditions have also changed. The information below explains how some things have changed during the past 80 years. Do workers today enjoy better or worse working conditions than their great-grandparents might have done?

**Clothing** – people have always needed suitable clothing for different jobs, but today there is more protective clothing available. For example, construction workers wear hard hats, police can wear bullet-proof jackets and health care workers often use rubber gloves.

**Hours worked** – on average, people in employment work shorter hours than they did 80 years ago, and are entitled to more holidays.

**Benefits** – unemployment benefits were first introduced during the 1920s. This was followed by laws on sick pay, state pensions and maternity leave.

**Children** – 80 years ago, many children were allowed to leave school and start full-time work at 14 or earlier. Today, you cannot leave school and be employed full-time until you are 16.

**Employment laws** – the 1920s saw the introduction of the first modern employment laws. Before this, workers had very few rights. Today, there are many laws on working conditions. For example, employees should have regular breaks, work within reasonable noise levels, and be safe at work. Laws also protect employees against discrimination on the grounds of race or sex, and against unfair dismissal.

**4.** Imagine if a worker today could travel back in time and talk to someone doing a similar job 80 years ago. Decide what the job would be, then write or role-play the conversation they might have about how the job and the working conditions have changed.

ROLE–PLAY

**5.** Predictions suggest that by the year 2030 more people will be working from home and people will be working shorter hours. If this comes true, how will it affect your working life and your leisure time?

CONSIDER

*bjective*
● To explore the reasons for having girlfriends and boyfriends and the pressures involved.

# Boyfriends, girlfriends

1. Make a list of reasons why some people of your age like to have a boyfriend or a girlfriend.

**BRAINSTORM**

2. Working in a small, single-sex group (all boys or all girls), brainstorm the qualities you think the ideal boyfriend should have and the qualities you think the ideal girlfriend should have. For example, you may have 'sense of humour' in both your lists. When you have finished brainstorming, choose the top five qualities from your list that you think are most important for a boyfriend to have, and do the same for a girlfriend.

**COMPARE**

3. As a class, compare your 'top five qualities'. Be prepared to explain your decisions and if your 'boyfriends' list was different from your 'girlfriends' list, explain why.

4. Read the problem page letters below and on page 13. What advice would you give in each case?

Dear Kerri,

My boyfriend and I have been together for a year and we have a great time. We both love football, swimming and the telly and we spend most of our spare time together with friends or just on our own. Recently, we have become very physical, kissing, cuddling and touching each other all over. So far we haven't had sex because it's such a big step but we both agree that we would like to. The problem is that I know my mum would be angry and upset if she found out we were having sex. She thinks we are much too young and also it's illegal because we are both only 15. I don't want to get my boyfriend into trouble and I don't want to do something I might regret but it's getting hard to stop ourselves from going any further. Do you think we should just go ahead, or would it be wrong?

Becky.

'Going out with', 'going steady', 'seeing', 'going with', 'walking out with' and 'courting' are all phrases that have been used to describe boyfriend and girlfriend relationships.

**KEY WORDS**   relationship   pressure   sexual feelings   crush

Dear Kerri,

I am 13 and my girlfriend is 14. I thought we were getting on fine but now she wants us to start having sex and she keeps asking me when we will do it. I know she had sex with her last boyfriend, and all our friends keep asking if we've done it yet. It also feels like every time I watch telly or read a magazine there are couples having sex. I tried to explain that I don't want to yet, but she got upset and said that I don't really love her. I do love her. How can I make her understand that I just don't feel ready? My friends think I'm just too scared. Maybe I am. Please tell me what to do.

Gopal

**5.** Sex is only one of the pressures young people in relationships may face. What other pressures and problems can having a boyfriend or girlfriend bring? Are there any pressures in not having a boyfriend or girlfriend?

**DISCUSS**

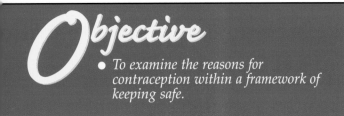
# Keeping safe – contraception

**1.** There are many things you need to know about before you start having sex and one of them is contraception. If you learn about it now, you will be prepared for the time when you are in a steady, loving relationship involving sex. Contraception, also called birth control or family planning, means the use of artificial methods to prevent pregnancy. Match each letter in the pictures below with the correct name. Write your answers in a chart.

| Letter | Image |
|--------|-------|
| a | Femidom |
| b | |

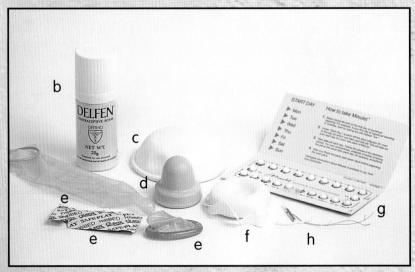

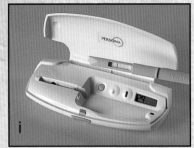

cervical cap    condom    contraceptive pill    diaphragm
emergency contraception (morning after pill)    Femidom    IUD    spermicidal foam
sponge    test for hormone levels (natural method)

**FACT TO THINK ABOUT … FACT TO THINK ABOUT … FACT TO THINK ABOUT …**

In England, a doctor can prescribe contraceptives to a girl under the age of 16 without telling her parents, as long as the doctor believes that the girl is mature enough to know what she is doing.

**KEY WORDS**  |  contraceptive   family planning   pregnant   sexually transmitted infection

**2.** Using the same format as below, produce another chart about all the contraceptives listed in the last activity.

| Name | Condom, also called sheath, Johnny, or rubber. |
|---|---|
| What is it? | A thin rubber sheath. |
| Where can you get it from? | Shops, supermarkets, machines in public toilets, family planning clinics. |
| How do you use it? | You pinch the end to make sure the tip isn't full of air, then roll it over the man's erect penis before intercourse. After intercourse, it has to be removed and thrown away. |
| How does it prevent pregnancy? | The sperm collects in the end of the condom and so cannot enter the woman's cervix. |
| Does it help prevent the spread of infection? | Yes. |
| What can go wrong? | Condoms can break occasionally and then there is no protection against pregnancy or infection. |

**3.** There is a lot of publicity about teenage pregnancies, but the truth is that unplanned pregnancies don't just happen to teenagers. In one antenatal class of 20 women whose ages ranged from 20 to 37, seven of the women admitted that their pregnancy was unplanned. List the reasons someone might give for not using contraception or failing to use it properly. What advice would you give them in each case?

**CONSIDER**

**4.** Any contraceptive can sometimes fail, and the only sure way of not getting pregnant and not catching sexually transmitted infections is not to have sex. That's why you need to think seriously before you have sex. Write a leaflet for young people thinking about starting a sexual relationship, giving advice on all the things they need to consider first. Remember to talk about feelings and emotions as well as facts.

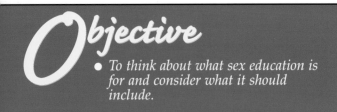

**Objective**

• To think about what sex education is for and consider what it should include.

# Thinking about sex education

**CONSIDER**

1. What do you understand by the term 'Sex education'? Think about the sex education you have had so far, both in school and out. Where has most of it come from? How useful has it been?

2. Read the viewpoints below, then say whether or not you agree with each one, and why. Why do people have different views on sex education?

> Sex education should be taught in school because everyone needs to know about it and your parents don't always tell you everything.

> Parents should teach about sex, not schools. That way they can teach children their values as well as the facts about what sex is. If children learn it in school, the teacher or other children might give them ideas that parents might not agree with.

> I think it's right that schools teach sex education. I was never taught about sex at school or at home and all I knew was what friends told me – most of which was wrong. I had a real shock when I got married.

> Schools don't teach enough sex education. They teach you the facts, but they don't talk enough about what it feels like or when you should or shouldn't have sex.

Studies in Holland have shown that the numbers of unplanned pregnancies can be drastically cut by effective sex education.

**KEY WORDS** | sex education    sexuality

**IMAGINE**

**3.** Imagine you have been asked to plan the curriculum for sex education. Write an outline showing what you would teach in each of the ages shown below.

> Ages 5 to 7                    Ages 7 to 11
> Ages 11 to 14                  Ages 14 to 16

**4.** Diewke and Henk live in Holland. Read their comments. What do they tell you about sex education in Holland? Is it the same, similar or very different from the sex education you have had? Give reasons for your answer.

We learn about sex at school but we also talk about it at home. My parents ask me about what I have learned at school and I can ask them about anything I don't understand. My mum and dad don't always agree – like when we talked about masturbation. My dad said he thought boys masturbated more than girls but my mum said it depended on the individual. I'm glad I can talk about sex with my parents.

At school we learn all the facts about sex, contraception, pregnancy, sexually transmitted infections and so on. We talk about feelings too. When I was on an exchange visit to England, I was in a sex education lesson where the teacher did most of the talking. She said it was normal for teenagers to have a crush on someone of the same sex and then she began talking about something else. In my school, we would have discussed it and people would have talked about crushes they had had.

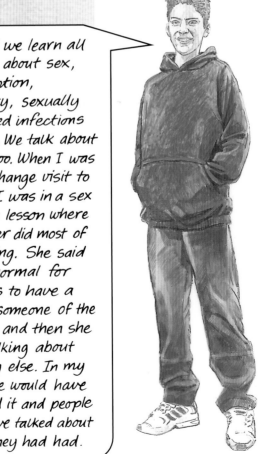

**5.** Write a statement saying what you think the aim of sex education should be.

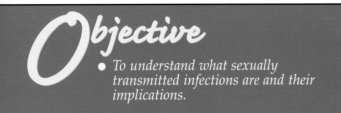

# Sexually transmitted infections

**CONSIDER**

1. Infections can be passed on in many ways, for example, coughing, sneezing, touching, kissing or sharing food. Some infections can be passed on during sexual intercourse and these are called 'sexually transmitted infections' or 'STI's'. People often talk about their health, but many people are reluctant to talk about STIs. Why don't people like to talk about STIs? What are the dangers of not talking about them?

2. Now do the following quiz to find out about STIs. When you have finished, check your answers as a class.

 **QUIZ**

a. Which of the following can be caught through sexual intercourse? Clamydia, pubic lice, syphilis, herpes, HIV, genital warts, gonorrhoea, trichomonas vaginalis, Fibonacci series.

b. Answer true or false to the following statements:
   i. If you had an STI you would be sore in the genital area.
   ii. If you had an STI you would need to go to the toilet more often than usual.
   iii. Rashes, itchiness, sores, blisters, pain in the genital area, a burning sensation when passing urine or having sex and an unusual discharge from the vagina or penis are all possible symptoms of STIs.
   iv. You can't get an STI if you stay with the same partner.
   v. STIs can be cured if they are treated quickly.

c. What should someone do if they think they may have an STI?

3. Look at the people on page 19 and say which of the following categories they come under:
   ● Safe from STIs.
   ● Some risk of getting STIs.
   ● Higher risk of getting STIs.

**KEY WORDS**   sexually transmitted infection   promiscuous   discharge   symptoms

**4.** Design a leaflet for people of your own age giving them information and advice about STIs.

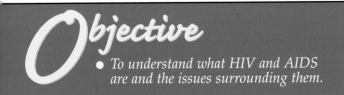

# HIV and AIDS –
## What's the difference?

**1.** People often mix up the terms HIV and AIDS. Read the definitions below to find out what they stand for.

### HIV – Human Immunodeficiency Virus

This is a virus that can be passed on through sexual intercourse. It can also be passed on by contaminated blood, for example, if you inject yourself with a needle that someone else has already used. A pregnant woman with HIV can pass the virus on to her unborn baby or to her baby through breastfeeding. Eventually, the virus stops a person's immune system from working, which means that their body can no longer fight other infections. If someone has contracted HIV, they are said to be 'HIV positive'. Someone who is HIV positive may not appear to be ill at all.

### AIDS – Acquired Immune Deficiency Syndrome

A syndrome is a collection of symptoms that, together, indicate that someone has a particular condition. Someone who is HIV positive will eventually become ill. They begin to catch infections that they cannot fight, and they become more and more ill. When this happens they are said to have AIDS. Someone can be HIV positive for a long time, as long as ten years, before developing AIDS. In the past, once someone developed AIDS they often died quite quickly. Today, there are better medical techniques that can help people with AIDS fight infections and survive for longer, but there is still no known cure.

**CONSIDER**

**2.** Read the above definitions again, then say whether each of the statements below is true or false.
- **a.** Someone who is HIV positive will appear to be very ill.
- **b.** You cannot catch AIDS.
- **c.** You can catch HIV.
- **d.** HIV can be spread through sexual intercourse.
- **e.** You cannot tell whether or not someone is HIV positive by looking at them.
- **f.** 'HIV positive' and 'HIV negative' mean the same thing.

**FACT TO THINK ABOUT ... FACT TO THINK ABOUT ... FACT TO THINK ABOUT ...**

The highest risk age group for contracting HIV is 15 to 24. More than a third of known cases fall within this age group.

**KEY WORDS** | AIDS   HIV positive   virus   immune system

**ROLE–PLAY**

**3.** Someone who suspects they may have contracted HIV should see a doctor straight away. Tests can show whether or not they have the virus. If they have, drugs can be used to help keep them well for longer, even if they do not have any symptoms to begin with. It is also important to know if you are HIV positive so that you can warn past sexual partners and protect future ones. Role-play a conversation with someone who thinks they might be HIV positive but is too scared to see a doctor.

**4.** The cartoons below all show some of the things that people may believe about HIV that are not true. In pairs, role-play conversations with the characters in the cartoons where one of you explains to the character that they are wrong. Take it in turns to be the one doing the explaining.

**5.** Design a poster explaining about HIV and AIDS to people of your age.

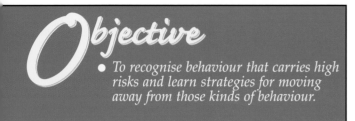

*Objective*
- To recognise behaviour that carries high risks and learn strategies for moving away from those kinds of behaviour.

# High-risk behaviour

**CONSIDER**

1. Look at the following UK laws. Do you think they are reasonable? Would you change any? Give reasons for your answers.

> A girl must be 16 to consent to sex. Under this age, she cannot legally consent to sex and any male having a sexual relationship with her is committing an offence.

> The age of consent does not apply to young boys.

> A girl under 16 can be prescribed contraception by her doctor without her parents' knowledge if the doctor believes that she is mature enough to know what she is doing.

> Lesbian relationships are not illegal, although, in practice, an older woman involved with a girl under the age of 16 may well be charged with indecent assault.

> Homosexual relationships are legal over the age of 16.

2. Where do you get information about puberty from? Which of these sources are reliable? (In other words – are likely to give you true facts.)

**DISCUSS**

3. Sexual relationships carry risks. Look at each of the characters on page 23. For each one, talk about what risks they have taken and what the consequences have been, or might be. How could these characters have reduced or removed the risks?

**FACT TO THINK ABOUT ... FACT TO THINK ABOUT ... FACT TO THINK ABOUT ...**

One adult interviewed about the lives of young people said, "Children today have hardly any childhood – there is too much sex pushed at them so they go out and do it."

**KEY WORDS** | high risk | promiscuous | sexually transmitted infection | rent boy | prostitute

**a.** Luke was in love with Emma. When they had sex Luke felt it was something special. Emma has now finished the relationship and Luke knows she is sleeping with someone else. Luke feels betrayed because he thought he was special to Emma.

**b.** Tim has run away from home because his stepfather bullies and hits him. He has met a man who says he will give Tim £30 if he comes back to his flat to 'do him a favour'.

**c.** Mandy has had sex with several boys in her class and has got a reputation for being 'easy'.

**d.** Gina and Max are both 14. Gina has just discovered that she is pregnant by Max. The pregnancy was unplanned.

**e.** Sofia and Abid are alone together in the house for the first time. Neither of them has talked about 'how far' they plan to go.

**4.** Draw up a table showing high-risk kinds of behaviour and their possible consequences. You could begin with 'Women beginning to have sex at an early age – possible consequence – higher risk of developing cervical cancer.'

**5.** Write a set of guidelines for young people with the title 'safer sex, safer relationships'.

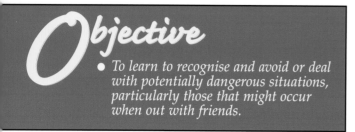

# Keeping safe — out and about

**CONSIDER**

**1.** How do you behave when you are out with your family? How do you behave when you are out with your friends? When are you more likely to take risks, and why?

**2.** Look at the headlines below. Choose one and invent the story that might be behind it.

> ### 14-year-old boy drowns in pond

> ### Six teenagers die in house fire

> ### 12-year-old girl missing – police fear abduction

> ### Girl dies in train track tragedy

> ### Alcohol poisoning claims life of 13-year-old

> ### Boy, 13, found dead outside nightclub

**DISCUSS**

**3.** Share some of your stories as a class. For each story, talk about what the person did that was risky and how he or she might have avoided what happened.

**4.** The headlines are all about young people who were killed. What other kinds of harm might a young person come to when they are out and about? What might the effect of some of these things be? How could they be avoided?

**FACT TO THINK ABOUT ... FACT TO THINK ABOUT ... FACT TO THINK ABOUT ...**

Over the past ten years, nine children, one as young as two, have been killed when goalposts fell on them.

| KEY WORDS | sexual abuse   abduction   hazard |
|---|---|

**5.** Jess was out with a group of friends when something terrible happened to her. She has not been able to tell anyone but this is what she wrote in her diary.

> Today has been the worst day of my life. I hope I die in my sleep. We all went to the youth club as usual and had a great time. Lynn's dad was taking us home but when we got outside it was Paul, her older brother, who was in the car. He dropped the other two off first, and then he dropped Lynn off because he said he was going on to a friend's house after he'd taken me home. On the way to my house, he took a side turning and stopped at the car park in the woods. I can't describe what happened. He told me that if I didn't let him do what he wanted he would tell everyone I'd done it anyway, but that wasn't what stopped me from saying 'no'. I was just too scared. He seemed so much older and bigger and I wasn't sure what he was going to do. You couldn't call it rape because I didn't even struggle. I just sort of froze. He drove me home as if nothing had happened. I said goodnight to Mum and went straight to my room. I don't know what to do. I wish he was dead. I wish I was dead.

Could Jess have avoided this situation? Is she right in saying 'you couldn't call it rape'? What might happen to Jess as a result of this incident? What should she do now?

**6.** No one wants to frighten young people into staying at home all the time but the fact is that there are risks that you need to think about when you are going out with friends. Put together a five-point plan that would help to keep a young person safe when he or she is out with friends.

**PLAN**

25

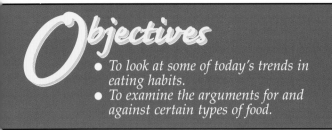

**Objectives**
- To look at some of today's trends in eating habits.
- To examine the arguments for and against certain types of food.

# Habits for a lifetime

**1.** The people below come from a school that has just had two cold drinks machines installed. The machines are very popular with most pupils and some of the staff, who use them frequently, but not everyone is happy with them. Read the comments below.

> The machines are a really good idea. We've had really hot weather recently and it's good to be able to go and buy a drink at break time. You need drinks during the day. Not everyone likes water and there aren't enough drinking fountains. I don't like the drinking fountains anyway. I think they're unhygienic because people put their mouths right over them.

> As a governor, I voted for the drinks machines. The money we raise from them can be used towards books and other resources.

> The drinks machines set a terrible example to pupils. All the drinks are fizzy, sugary drinks containing lots of chemicals, apart from the diet varieties, which are fizzy drinks with no sugar but even more chemicals. Some of the parents have complained and, as a teacher, I have certainly noticed a change in the behaviour of some of the pupils. Some of them arrive in lessons 'wound up' and overexcited because of the raised sugar levels caused by the drinks. Others are spending all their money on drinks and are having no lunch at midday. Several of the parents have complained. I think the machines should be removed.

**CONSIDER**

**2.** Do you think the drinks machines are a good idea? Write a letter to the school governors saying whether or not you think the machines should stay and giving your reasons.

Some medical experts predict that, if current trends continue, half the population will be clinically obese by the year 2030.

| KEY WORDS | fast foods | healthy eating | nutrition |
| --- | --- | --- | --- |

**3.** Many school canteens these days have been redesigned to look more like 'fast food' outlets. They often sell 'fast foods' as well, such as chips, burgers, sausages and pizzas. Although most canteens still offer a 'healthy' option, the fast foods are usually more popular. Look at the three menus below. Take a vote to find out which menu would be most popular in your class. Which one provides a healthier meal? Why?

Shepherd's pie,
cabbage,
carrots,
boiled potatoes.
Steam pudding
and custard.
Water.

Vegetable and pasta bake with crunchy cheese topping.

—

Broccoli or side salad.
Yoghurt or fresh fruit.

—

Fruit juice or carton of milk.

BURGER, CHIPS, PEAS OR BEANS.

CHOCOLATE CRISPY CAKE. ORANGE JUICE OR MILK SHAKE.

**4.** Brainstorm the benefits of eating a healthy diet, and the dangers of eating an unhealthy diet.

> **BRAINSTORM**

**5.** Government research shows that many people who know all about the importance of a healthy diet continue to eat unhealthily much of the time. Produce a report for the Government exploring the reasons why many people do not eat healthily and outlining steps that could be taken to encourage them to change their habits. You may have to carry out further research or surveys to help you compile your report.

**6.** Should the Government try to persuade people to eat more healthily or should people be left to eat what they want?

> **CONSIDER**

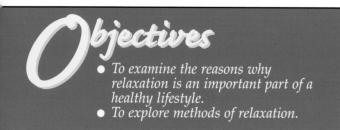

*Objectives*

- *To examine the reasons why relaxation is an important part of a healthy lifestyle.*
- *To explore methods of relaxation.*

# Learning to relax

**CONSIDER**

**1.** Which of the following body signs would someone under stress show, and which would someone who was relaxed show?

| | | |
|---|---|---|
| increased blood pressure | lowered blood pressure | increased rate of breathing |
| sweating | increased muscle tension | slower breathing |
| increased heart rate | reduced muscle tension | |

Read the doctor's opinion given below:

Stress can be a positive force. If you are worried about an exam, you may be more likely to study for it. If you are frightened of being attacked in an alley you may choose to avoid it.

Stress is also an important part of relationships. Love, anger, lust and excitement can all be stressful experiences but most people would not choose to live entirely without them.

Stress in your life needs to be balanced by relaxation. What you do to relax may not actually 'relax' your body. Sport involves placing the body under stress but we call it relaxing because it enables a person to forget about other things, feel physically fit and have fun. Going to see a film may be 'stressful' if it is a horror film, but it is also 'relaxing' if you enjoy it and come out feeling that you have had a good time.

**2.** Divide a piece of paper into two columns. In one column, list things you find stressful and, in the other, list things you find relaxing. Which ones have you done in the last week? Do you think you have had a good balance of relaxation and stress? (A good balance is what feels right for you – you may not have done the same number of each.)

**FACT TO THINK ABOUT ... FACT TO THINK ABOUT ... FACT TO THINK ABOUT ...**

Less than 20 per cent of people are effective in the face of a crisis such as a fire or flood.

**KEY WORDS** | relaxation   stress   calmness

**3.** The people below are talking about their relaxation habits. How would you feel about each of the activities? Give reasons for your answers.

> I practise yoga. It is a form of stretching and standing in special ways that also uses meditation and breathing techniques. I find it calming, it helps me focus and it keeps my body supple and balanced.

> I use a breathing technique that I learned when I was pregnant. You just stop what you are doing and breathe slowly. Breathe in for a count of four, pause for whatever feels comfortable, breathe out for a count of four, pause, then start again. However stressed I am, if I breathe like this for a few moments, I relax almost immediately. It really works. Try it!

> I use aromatherapy and visualisation. I choose a time when I won't be disturbed and get myself comfortable. I burn oils that are known for their calming properties, and I close my eyes and breathe slowly. Then I picture myself somewhere calm and relaxing, perhaps on a beach, in a meadow, or walking through a shady forest. I see myself as happy, relaxed and at peace with the world. When I have finished, I am left with a huge feeling of peace and joy.

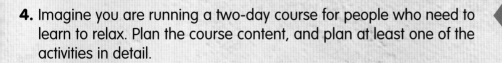

**IMAGINE**

**4.** Imagine you are running a two-day course for people who need to learn to relax. Plan the course content, and plan at least one of the activities in detail.

**5.** Write an advert for your course. Remember to include the reasons why learning to relax is so important.

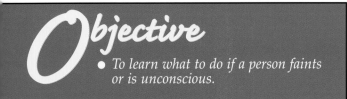

# Emergency aid

**CONSIDER**

1. Read the explanations of fainting and unconsciousness. What things might make a person faint? What things might make a person unconscious?

## Fainting

'Fainting' is the term used to describe a brief loss of consciousness caused by a temporary lack of blood to the brain. The patient often feels 'faint' before fainting, and may feel dizzy, sick or have disturbances of vision. Someone who faints will fall over. This helps restore the blood flow to the head and the person usually recovers quickly.

## Unconsciousness

A person who loses consciousness for anything more than a few seconds needs medical attention. A person who is completely unconscious will not respond if you speak to them or shake them gently. There are different levels of consciousness and a person may groan or try to move, but if they are unable to communicate or move themselves much they are still in a serious condition needing medical attention.

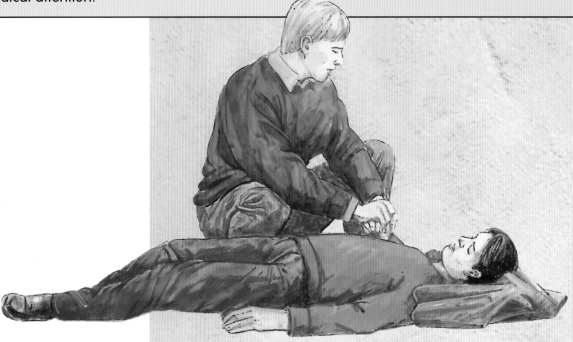

2. A person who has fainted needs the blood supply restored to the head, a good supply of oxygen, and reassurance. Using this information, write out guidelines for dealing with a person who has fainted.

If you are alone with a small child who becomes unconscious and there is a phone nearby, it is better to take them to the phone to call for help than to leave them alone. That way you will be able to answer any questions and follow any instructions you are given over the phone.

**KEY WORDS**   faint   unconsciousness   emergency   recovery position

**3.** Someone who is unconscious but breathing should be placed in the recovery position. Look at the picture of someone being placed in the recovery position below. Why is it a good position in which to lay an unconscious person? Practise putting each other in this position by following the instructions. The casualty begins on his or her back. Remember, they are 'unconscious' so don't drop their head or hurt them.

**a.** Kneel beside the casualty, remove any spectacles or anything tight across the chest or throat.

**b.** Straighten the casualty's legs.

**c.** Place the arm nearest to you out at right angles to the body, elbow bent, palm uppermost.

**d.** Bring the far arm across the chest. Place hand, palm downwards, near cheek.

**e.** Grasp the far thigh. Bend knee up, keeping the foot flat on the ground.

**f.** Keeping the hand pressed against the cheek, pull at the thigh to roll the casualty towards you on to his or her side.

**g.** Tilt head back slightly to keep airways open. Adjust hand if necessary to keep head in position.

**h.** Adjust upper leg if necessary, so that hip and knee are bent at right angles.

**4.** Imagine you are at a party when someone collapses. The person is breathing with difficulty. In groups, decide what you would do. Compare your answers with those of other groups and make a class decision on the best plan of action.

**IMAGINE**

31

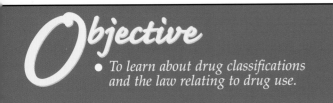

# Knowing the law

1. In the UK, there are two main categories of drug offences. Read about them in the boxes below.

**Possession:** This means being caught with a small amount of an illegal drug or drugs that you are likely to use for yourself.

**Possession with intent to supply:** This means being caught with an illegal drug or drugs that you may be planning to pass on to other people. The amount may still be small and, even if you are giving the drug away and not charging for it, the offence is still possession with intent to supply. A few ecstasy tablets that you plan to share with your friends would be considered possession with intent to supply.

**CONSIDER**

2. Possession with intent to supply is punished more severely than possession. Why is this?

3. The Misuse of Drugs Act (1971) classifies drugs as class A, B or C, with class A drugs being considered the most dangerous. Class A drugs are often also ones that are very addictive. Class C drugs are considered less dangerous, but they can still be dangerous, particularly if they are used over a long period or at the same time as other drugs or alcohol. Look at the table below, then sort the list of drugs into class A, B or C. Check your answers with the answers at the back of this book.

| Drug classification | Maximum penalty for possession | Maximum penalty for possession with intent to supply |
|---|---|---|
| Class A | 7 years prison and/or fine | Life imprisonment and/or fine |
| Class B | 5 years prison and/or fine | 14 years prison and/or fine |
| Class C | 2 years prison and/or fine | 5 years prison and/or fine |

| crack | temazepam | cannabis | ecstasy | LSD |
prepared magic mushrooms | speed | cocaine | steroids |
speed prepared for injection | tranquillisers | heroin

The first reported death from ecstasy in the UK was in 1989. Over 70 young people have lost their lives through taking ecstasy since then.

**KEY WORDS**  Class A  Class B  Class C  possession  supply

**4.** Look at the cases below. For each one, decide whether or not any of the people involved has broken the law, and if so, in what way.

**a.** Gary, Frank and Jackie have been picking magic mushrooms. They are going to make a drink from them.

**b.** Bhavna and Shaun are smoking cannabis.

**c.** Pete has asked his younger sister Maria to go down the road to buy two ecstasy tablets from his friend.

**d.** Gareth's mother found him smoking cannabis in the house and threatened to go to the police. He promised he wouldn't do it again and she agreed to forget the incident.

**5.** Check your answers as a class. Which offence would be likely to carry the highest penalty?

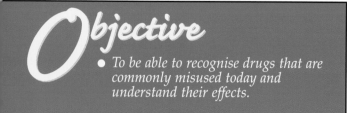
# Recognising drugs

**1.** The drugs below are all drugs that you may come across at some stage. It is important that you are able to recognise a drug and what it does.

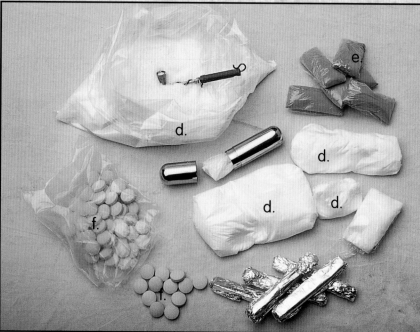

**FACT TO THINK ABOUT … FACT TO THINK ABOUT … FACT TO THINK ABOUT …**

Some suppliers have sold dog worming tablets to people who believed they were buying ecstasy.

| KEY WORDS | effect   addiction   overdose |
|-----------|-------------------------------|

Match the name of each drug with its street names and picture.
Write your answers in a chart and check your answers as a class.

| cannabis | cocaine or crack | ecstasy |
|----------|------------------|---------|
| heroin   | LSD              | amphetamines |

**Street names**
i  – speed, whizz, uppers, amph, Billy, sulphate
ii – coke, Charlie, snow, C
iii – marijuana, draw, blow, weed, puff, shit, hash, ganja
iv – smack, brown, horse, gear, H, junk, scag, jack
v  – E, XTC, doves, disco biscuits, echoes, hug drug, eccies,
    burgers, fantasy, MDMA
vi – acid, trips, tabs, blotters, microdots, dots

| Letter | Drug | Street name |
|--------|------|-------------|
| a. | cannabis or marijuana | (iii) marijuana, draw, blow … |
| b. |  |  |

**IMAGINE**

**2.** Read the information in the charts on pages 76–77. Imagine you were talking to someone who had tried one of the drugs described a few times. On your own, write down what they say about why they used it and how it made them feel, but don't mention the name of the drug.

**3.** In pairs, read each other's writing and try to identify which drug your partner has been writing about.

**4.** Write a story about someone who has been taking illegal drugs for a long time. You could end your story with the words, 'I wish I'd never … '.

# Objective

● To raise awareness of our roles as consumers and find out about the laws in this area.

# Consumer power

1. Young people are big business. Every week in the UK, young people under 16 spend around £73 000 000. Some businesses, such as canned drinks, rely heavily on young people's custom. Shops and services have to abide by the law when selling goods. There is a lot to know about buying goods. Use the information below to help you with the rest of the tasks in this unit.

When you buy goods, the law says that the goods must be:
● of satisfactory quality
● fit for their purpose
● as described.

You have no grounds for complaint if:
● you were told about the fault when you bought the item
● you damaged the item yourself
● the goods are fine, but you have changed your mind about them; however, many shops will allow you a refund or to exchange items
● the goods don't fit; again, most shops will let you have a refund or exchange goods if you have the receipt.

If you are unhappy with goods or services, you should go back to the shop or service provider. Remember:
● If you are returning goods, you must return them in the same condition they were sold in, and as quickly as is reasonably possible. If you cannot get back to the shop within about a week, you should telephone them to let them know there is a problem. You do not have to return goods at your own expense, the seller should pay for collection. (In practice of course it is much easier to take small items back yourself.)
● Legally, you do not have to show the receipt for the goods; you still have the same rights without it. In practice, it is better to have the receipt because this proves that you bought the goods from that shop.
● You have the same rights over goods bought in a sale as non-sale items.
● If you suffer loss or injury because of faulty goods or services then you may be able to claim compensation.

**CONSIDER**

2. Which of the products below break the law, and how?
a. A pair of trainers advertised as 'fully air-cushioned'. When you get home, you discover that there is only one air pocket in the heel.
b. You give the shopkeeper details of your computer and he says the game you are buying will run on it. When you get home, the game won't run.
c. You buy a top advertised as 'cotton rich'. When you get it home, you discover that it is 75 per cent cotton and 25 per cent polyester.
d. You wear some new shoes at school but, after a week, the strap breaks. The shop says that they were 'fashion shoes', designed for occasional wear only.

**FACT TO THINK ABOUT ... FACT TO THINK ABOUT ... FACT TO THINK ABOUT ...**

A recent survey shows that 60 per cent of 13-year-olds have a television in their bedroom and over 30 per cent have a video player.

**KEY WORDS**  consumer  product  goods  service  buyer  seller

**3.** Imagine you have bought the goods or services shown below. Role-play a situation where you try to sort out the problem. Take it in turns to be the person doing the complaining, and make some of the shopkeepers more helpful than others! Be warned – in one situation you are not entitled to your money back!

**IMAGINE**

**a.** You bought a book and then discovered that some of the pages were printed upside down. You have lost the receipt but you know this was the shop you bought it in.

**b.** You had your hair coloured at the hairdressers. The next day, your scalp was itchy and sore and you had to go to the doctors. You have gone back to the hairdressers to complain.

**c.** You bought a pair of trousers and when you got them home there was a button missing. You wore them that night anyway, and washed them. You're now trying to get your money back.

**d.** You bought a television for your room and it has stopped working. You cannot get it back to the shop so you phone them.

**4.** Design a leaflet for young people about their rights when buying goods and services. Your leaflet should include a section of advice on what to do if you are unhappy about a product or service.

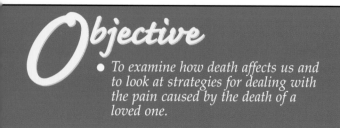

# Dealing with death

**Objective**

- To examine how death affects us and to look at strategies for dealing with the pain caused by the death of a loved one.

**CONSIDER**

1. Take a few quiet moments and write down your thoughts about death. You do not need to write in sentences and you do not need to show anyone what you have written if you don't want to.

**DISCUSS**

2. As a class, talk about some of the thoughts you had in your quiet moment. You do not need to share anything you want to keep private but you will probably find that some people in the group will want to share things.

3. Losing a parent is always hard, and it is especially hard if you are still young yourself. Look at the story of Amy and her mother. List the things that helped Amy prepare for her mother's death.

When Amy was nine, her mother was diagnosed with bowel cancer. Amy and her mother lived alone so Amy went to stay with friends while her mother was in hospital. Her mother always told her the truth about what the doctors said and what was happening. Amy's mother recovered, and life returned to normal for another two years.

When Amy was almost 12, her mother fell ill again, this time with liver cancer. She had treatment that left her feeling very ill and the doctors said she probably had less than a year to live. Amy's mother didn't tell Amy she was dying but she did say there was a chance she wouldn't get well and they had better make plans.

It was decided that Amy would eventually live with her aunt's family who lived about 60 miles away. Amy began to visit her aunt regularly and to stay whenever her mother was in hospital. She had to share a room with her 15-year-old cousin, Emma, but it was redecorated and some of Amy's things were moved in so that she would feel at home.

Amy's mother had several months of feeling quite well. During this time, Amy lived at home and they sometimes talked about what life would be like for Amy in the future. Gradually, Amy understood that her mum was dying. Together they made a special box for Amy. Inside it were photos, letters and jewellery of her mum's, a favourite scarf, and other personal items to help Amy remember the happy times. Amy's mum has also written a letter for when Amy is 18, although Amy doesn't know this yet.

**KEY WORDS** | death  mourning  grave  life

Amy tried not to think about the future but she did sometimes talk to her friends. She knew that she would have to change schools when her mum died and she felt guilty because this upset her as much as the thought of her mum dying.
The school year finished and Amy and her mum had a quiet summer. They spent days painting together, watching films and cooking. Towards the end, Amy's mum had a few bad days. Amy spent a weekend with her aunt and her aunt asked her if she would like to move in with them now, ready for the new school year. Amy talked it over with her mum and decided that it would be for the best. She felt terrible leaving her mum but at the same time she felt a great relief to be living in a house where everything was normal.
Amy visited her mum two or three times a week. By Christmas, her mum was very ill and moved into a hospice near Amy's aunt so Amy was able to visit every day. The staff at the hospice talked to Amy and she also talked to the rabbi.
When Amy's mum slipped into a coma the hospice called Amy and she went with her aunt to see her mother for the last time. Amy was walking round the garden of the hospice when the nurse came to say that her mother had died.

**4.** Choose three points in the story and write a diary entry for Amy, her mother or both.

**5.** What things could help Amy cope with her mother's death now that she has gone?

CONSIDER

39

# Marriage

**Objective**
- *To understand the role and importance of marriage in today's society.*

1. You may have heard people say that marriage is out of date these days, but the fact is that more than 85 per cent of adults get married at some point in their lives. Brainstorm the reasons why people get married.

2. Marriage is still very popular, but some of the traditions associated with marriage have changed. Look at each of the examples below and say what they tell you about the changes that have happened in society.

A white wedding dress once symbolised that the bride was a virgin in Western cultures. White dresses are still popular, but many brides choose other colours.

In several cultures, it is traditional for the father to 'give away' the bride, which comes from the idea that the father 'owned' his daughter until her new husband takes over this responsibility.

Many years ago, nearly all weddings were religious ceremonies. Today, almost 50 per cent of couples marry somewhere other than a religious building, in secular (non-religious) services.

The Christian marriage service used to use the words 'obey' and 'worship'. Today, couples can choose to use the word 'respect' instead.

**FACT TO THINK ABOUT ... FACT TO THINK ABOUT ... FACT TO THINK ABOUT ...**

Some same-sex couples choose to go through the equivalent of a marriage ceremony.

**KEY WORDS**    marriage    virgin    vows    register office    religious ceremony    civil ceremony

**3.** Many couples choose a civil marriage ceremony rather than a religious ceremony. This can be held in a register office or other place that has permission to hold wedding ceremonies, such as a town hall, hotel or other building. Sometimes couples choose to write their own marriage vows. Write a set of marriage vows that could be used by a couple wishing to show their love and commitment to each other. They may be religious or non-religious.

**4.** Read the views on marriage given below. Discuss each one and say whether you agree or disagree.

**DISCUSS**

> Marriage ties you to someone and then it can be terrible going through a divorce. It's much better to live with a person. Then, if the relationship breaks down, you can both move on to something new.

> Marriage shows that you are committed to making the relationship work. If you're not married, it's too easy to give up when things get difficult. If you're married, you're more likely to try to solve problems and work through the difficult times.

> Marriage is the best basis for having children. It provides a stable background and gives the children a feeling of security.

> Marriage is just a piece of paper. It doesn't change how you feel about someone. If you really love someone, it doesn't matter if you're married or not and if you don't, a piece of paper won't make you love them.

**5.** Write a statement summing up your beliefs about marriage.

*Objective*
- To explore the nature and value of family life.

# Family life

1. 'Family' means different things to different people, but just about everyone has had experience of family life. You could say we are all experts. Begin by reading what the families below have to say.

**Mother:** I have always lived with my mother. She moved in with us when we got married. I am very lucky because it has meant I could carry on working, knowing that Tyan-yu would be safely looked after by my mother.

**Father:** We are modern Chinese, and my wife and I both make the decisions. Family life for me is about sharing.

**Grandmother:** It is a great privilege to watch my daughter turn into such a good wife and mother. I like to think that I have passed on some of my ways to her.

**Mother:** I am not like my mother at all. She thinks I go out too much or disagree with Rakesh. But family life is important to me and I carry on many of her traditions.

**Father:** It is a responsibility looking after this family, but it is also a joy. I love watching my children grow, even when they argue with me, it shows they have a strong spirit.

**Eldest child (female):** Mum and Dad are so old-fashioned, but Grandma wants me to do well. She says I am the new generation and encourages me to be independent. She is a great support to me.

**Grandmother:** We are always there for each other in times of trouble. Children learn respect in the family.

**FACT TO THINK ABOUT ... FACT TO THINK ABOUT ... FACT TO THINK ABOUT ...**

The philosopher Plato wrote around 300BC, 'The family must be abolished if men and women are to lead the same lives.'

**KEY WORDS** | family values   family life   'happy families'

**First child:** I will be leaving my family soon to go and find work. I am dreading it. I am so used to their company, their laughter and their concern for me.

**Boy:** I will also be leaving soon, but I am looking forward to it. It will be exciting. I am fed up with always having to explain where I am going or what I am doing. There is no privacy here. I do love my family, but it's time for me to see more of the world.

**Mum:** Since Edward died, I have brought the children up alone. They are hard work but they are also a great comfort to me. I worry that the boys don't have a father as a role model. I think Ella has had to grow up fast too. I don't know what I'd do without her really.

**Ella:** We have always been a close family, but I think I am even closer to Mum, now that Dad's not here. Sometimes, I wish I just lived alone for some peace and quiet. But I love my family. Losing a part of it makes you realise how special family is.

**CONSIDER**

2. What are the similarities and differences between the families shown here? What conclusions can you draw about family life from their comments?

3. Using ideas from the families on this page, together with your own ideas, make a list of things which could be considered 'family values'.

4. Some cultures celebrate a families day. Design a card and write a suitable message to celebrate the values of family life.

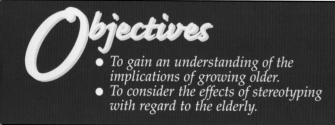

*Objectives*
- To gain an understanding of the implications of growing older.
- To consider the effects of stereotyping with regard to the elderly.

# Groups in society – the elderly

## BRAINSTORM

1. Brainstorm words you associate with the phrase 'elderly people'. Where does your image of elderly people come from?

2. Working in small groups, look at each of the facts below in turn and make notes about the implications of that fact, for example, what it means for the United Kingdom and what it means for individual people. Also jot down any questions that the fact raises, for example, you might ask why more elderly women live alone than men.

There are about 10.6 million people over the age of retirement in the UK. That's over 18 per cent of the population.

Almost three-quarters of people over the age of 85 are women.

The number of people of pensionable age in the UK is expected to be around 12 million by 2021.

The percentage of people of all ages who have a long-standing illness is 35 per cent. This rises to 59 per cent in the 65–74 age range, and 66 per cent in the over 75 age range.

The percentage of people who live alone over the age of 75 is 31 per cent of men and 58 per cent of women.

In England, approximately 198 000 people over the age of 65 live in registered retirement homes.

The chances of living in a long-stay hospital or care home by the age of 75 is 1 per cent, rising to 21.7 per cent over the age of 85.

In 1996, there were 5523 people over the age of 100. This figure is expected to rise to 39 000 by the year 2036.

## DISCUSS

3. Discuss your conclusions and your questions as a class. Which fact surprised you the most?

4. The media may influence our view of elderly people. Age Concern analysed over 3600 articles from national and local newspapers that mentioned elderly people. Read the comment on their findings:

# FACT TO THINK ABOUT ... FACT TO THINK ABOUT ... FACT TO THINK ABOUT ...

Michelangelo started his designs for St Peters in Rome at the age of 71.

**KEY WORDS**    elderly   retired   ageism   stereotype

> There are a large number of stories about older people and issues that concern them, such as pensions and the NHS. However, the press has not updated its view of older people, depicting them as victims - especially of crime. Stories about older people tend to use tired and predictable words and regard active older people as the exception, not the rule.

**5.** You are a reporter for a local newspaper. Your editor wants the newspaper to present a more up-to-date image of older people. Write a news story based on one of the following situations.

Mrs Emerson, aged 69, walks with a stick and is afraid of heights. She recently flew to Australia on her own and took a trip in a hot air balloon over the bushlands.

Coach driver Ron Wilson drove 50 elderly people on a day trip to Dorset. He followed them up the steep coastal path but fell and twisted his ankle and had to be helped down by two of the pensioners.

Sarah Dickens manages a company making car stereo speakers. Over 60 per cent of her employees are over the age of 60 because she believes they are more reliable, enthusiastic and experienced than younger employees.

Two teenagers have nominated their grandmother for an award to find the best elderly role model. They say she spends hours working for a local political party, often travelling to London for important meetings.

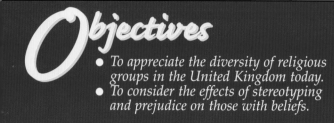

**O**bjectives

- To appreciate the diversity of religious groups in the United Kingdom today.
- To consider the effects of stereotyping and prejudice on those with beliefs.

# Groups in society – those with beliefs

**BRAINSTORM**

1. Brainstorm religions that are practised in the United Kingdom today. Why are there so many different forms of religion?

2. The people below all hold strong religious beliefs. What problems might they face as a result of these? Give examples and say how these problems might be overcome.

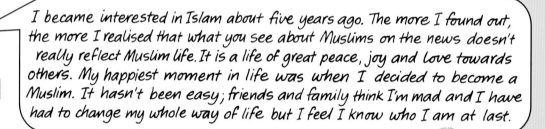

I became interested in Islam about five years ago. The more I found out, the more I realised that what you see about Muslims on the news doesn't really reflect Muslim life. It is a life of great peace, joy and love towards others. My happiest moment in life was when I decided to become a Muslim. It hasn't been easy; friends and family think I'm mad and I have had to change my whole way of life but I feel I know who I am at last.

I have always been interested in religion and I went to church with my family as a child. Then, I discovered Buddhism on a trip to Nepal and it felt like coming home. My family think it's just a phase but I know it has changed my life for ever.

I am a Hindu and a doctor. I get fed up with the ignorance people show. At work once I mentioned that I was hungry and a colleague asked, "Is it that Ramadan thing where you're not allowed to eat?" When I tried to explain that I wasn't a Muslim, he said, "I get all these funny religions mixed up."

I got some real stares when I first went to the church near our new house. People were very kind but they assumed I had just converted to Christianity. They were willing to learn though, and listened when I explained that many Indians are Christians, both here and in India. My family have been Christians for generations. They still think it's odd that I wear a sari. They don't understand that culture isn't the same as religion.

My friends all know I am a Sikh, but when we learned about Sikhs at school they all wanted to know why I didn't wear a turban. I tried to point out that people can make personal decisions within their religion. My religion is the central core to my life. It influences everything I do, but I don't feel I have to show an outward expression of it by wearing a turban.

**FACT TO THINK ABOUT ... FACT TO THINK ABOUT ... FACT TO THINK ABOUT ...**

Despite the decline in the number of people attending religious worship, in a recent survey, one in five people said they definitely believed in God, and one in ten said they definitely did not.

| **KEY WORDS** | faith   belief   religion   culture |
| --- | --- |

> My comedy act used to be full of jokes about Jews and I used to think that was OK because I am one. The trouble was that other people would tell me Jewish jokes that I found offensive. They couldn't see a difference between the jokes I told, about Jewish customs, and the jokes they told about Jews being worthless, mean or victims of racism. I told someone I found his joke offensive once and he apologised and said he thought I wouldn't mind because I wasn't a "real Jew". I'm not sure what he meant by that but I only tell Jewish jokes in front of Jewish audiences now.

**3.** All of the people above have faced criticism or prejudice as a result of their beliefs, yet they continue to practise their religion. Manraaj sums up their feelings when he says "My religion is the central core to my life." What does he mean by this? How might this belief affect his life?

**CONSIDER**

**4.** Role-play a television talk show that is exploring the lives of religious believers in the UK today. Try to include the following in your role-play:

**ROLE-PLAY**

- people with religious beliefs
- people without religious beliefs
- people who have been victims of violence or abuse because of their beliefs
- people who have abused or harmed religious believers.

Some of you could role-play the characters on this page. Take time deciding on what role you will play and thinking through the character before the role-play begins. You will need a strong 'host' or 'chairperson'. Brainstorm some questions to start the discussion before the role-play begins.

**5.** At the end of talk shows, the host often makes a statement about the subject that has been discussed. Write a statement summing up your views about religious belief in the United Kingdom today.

**Objective**
● To raise awareness of racism and develop strategies for combating it.

1. Racism means treating one group of people less favourably than another because of their colour, religious belief or ethnic origin. Discuss examples of racism you have seen or heard about. What happened? What was the outcome?

2. People who encourage racism usually use myths and lies to encourage others to be racist. The eight statements below contain four myths and four linked facts. Pair the statements and identify which is the myth and which is the fact.

There are too many coloured people in the UK today and they're taking over.

Black and Asian people are statistically more likely to be the victims of crime than white people.

Immigrants are all black or Asian. They are all poor and they want to get rich in Britain.

Black and Asian men are twice as likely to be unemployed as white men. 22 per cent of Pakistanis with 'A' levels or above are unemployed, only five per cent of white people with the same level of qualifications are unemployed.

Black people come over here and take our jobs.

63 per cent of immigrants to the UK are white. Many immigrants, including black and Asian immigrants, are professional people, which the UK needs.

**FACT TO THINK ABOUT ... FACT TO THINK ABOUT ... FACT TO THINK ABOUT ...**

It is estimated that there is one racial attack on a black or Asian person every 15 minutes in the UK.

**KEY WORDS** | racist   racism   discrimination   ethnic minority   equality

> Black and Asian people are responsible for most of the crime in the UK.

> Many people from ethnic minorities are white. Only five in every hundred people in the UK are black or Asian.

**ROLE–PLAY**

**3.** In pairs, role-play a conversation between someone who believes some of the racist myths above and another person who points out why they are wrong.

**4.** Many football clubs have joined the 'Kick Racism Out of Football' campaign. The box below shows some of the ways in which clubs are tackling racism. Read each point in turn and talk about why it is important and what the effects might be.

---

**Action plan for football clubs**

**a.** Print a statement in all match programmes and in posters around the ground saying that the club will not tolerate racism, and spelling out the action it will take against supporters who are involved in racist chanting or other racist behaviour.

**b.** Ban supporters involved in racist behaviour from the club.

**c.** Take action to prevent the sale or giving out of racist literature in or around the ground on match days.

**d.** Take disciplinary action against players who shout racist abuse.

**e.** Remove all racist graffiti from the ground as a matter of urgency.

**f.** Adopt an equal opportunities policy in the areas of employment and provision of services.

---

**5.** Design a poster suitable for a football ground showing the club's position on racism.

**6.** What would you do if someone told you a racist joke? What might be the consequences of your actions? Compare your answer with those of other people.

**CONSIDER**

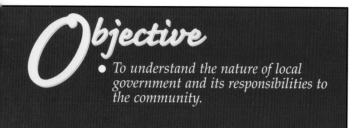

**O**bjective

● To understand the nature of local government and its responsibilities to the community.

# Local government

1. Imagine each of the decisions below has been made in your school. They could affect you. Who is most likely to have made each decision; the school governors, the headteacher, the class teacher or the students?

> **a.** You can choose who you work with when you are working in pairs.
> **b.** The school has some extra money that will be spent on a new science block.
> **c.** All lunchtime clubs must finish ten minutes before the end of lunchtime.
> **d.** A school council will be set up with one representative from every class.
> **e.** A new teacher has been taken on to teach drama.
> **f.** The lesson will begin with ten minutes silent reading.

2. The United Kingdom is a bit like your school, in that some decisions are made 'high up', and some are made on a more 'local' level. The UK National Government, based in London, makes many of the major decisions affecting the UK as a whole. Scotland, Wales and Northern Ireland have 'national' bodies that make some of the decisions and local government makes decisions locally, at town and county level. Just like your school, decisions are discussed. Decisions made on one level will affect the other levels. Local government can be organised in different ways. Read the examples below, then find out how local government is organised in your area.

I have a county council, which deals with things like schools, roads and social services. Then we have a smaller district council, which runs the sports centre and empties the dustbins.

My county council is in charge of all the local government services in my area.

**FACT TO THINK ABOUT ... FACT TO THINK ABOUT ... FACT TO THINK ABOUT ...**

Until 1995, most police forces came under the control of local government, but they are now independent authorities.

**KEY WORDS**  local government   councillor   services   elected   employee

**RESEARCH**

**3.** Local government is responsible for many of the services that you use. Produce a large poster or collage showing the range of local government services. You will need to carry out some research to find out what services are provided. The illustration below may give you some ideas about where to collect your information.

**CONSIDER**

**4.** Local government employs millions of people across the country, but the councillors who run the council and who make many of the decisions are elected volunteers. Why might someone stand as a councillor? What are the advantages of having elected councillors? Find out the names of your local councillors.

**5.** Councillors can decide what the priorities are in their local area. Create two lists showing the advantages and disadvantages of decisions being made locally.

*Objective*
- To understand the structure and role of the House of Commons.

# Inside the House of Commons

1. The floor plan on this page shows the House of Commons chamber. Read the labels below and talk about what each of the words in italic means (use a dictionary if you need to). Next, decide where each label goes on the floor plan. Check your answers as a class.

A. Table that stands between the benches.

B. Mace – this staff represents *Parliament's* authority. It is carried in during the opening of Parliament and must be on the table during debates.

C. Despatch boxes – these two boxes stand on the table. *Ministers* stand by them to speak.

D. The Speaker acts as chairperson in the chamber.

E. Government front bench, where *Government* ministers sit.

F. Opposition front bench, where the official *Opposition* 'shadow ministers' sit.

G. Backbenchers – *MPs* in the Government's *party* sit behind the Government front bench. MPs in the Opposition's party sit behind the Opposition front bench.

H. Other opposition parties – all MPs apart from those in the Government's party and the official Opposition's party sit here.

I. Press gallery – where reporters sit.

J. Public gallery – where members of the public sit.

K. Special galleries – peers, important visitors and diplomats sit here.

L. The Ayes lobby – when a *vote* is taken, MPs wishing to vote 'yes' go through a door into this room to be counted.

M. The Noes lobby. MPs wishing to vote 'no' go into this room.

N. Bar of the House. Only House of Commons MPs are allowed to cross this white line when the house is in session.

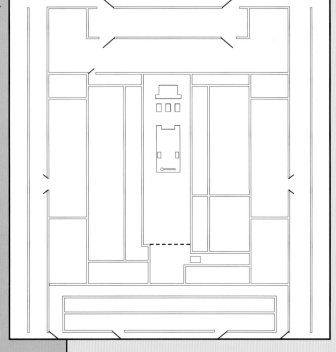

**CONSIDER**

2. Should Parliament be moved to a purpose-built, modern building? What advantages might there be to Parliament being in an historic building?

**FACT TO THINK ABOUT ... FACT TO THINK ABOUT ... FACT TO THINK ABOUT ...**

The 659 seats are divided up as follows:
529 for England; 40 for Wales; 72 for Scotland; 18 for Northern Ireland.

**KEY WORDS**  Parliament   Government   Opposition   Minister   front bench   back bench

**3.** The House of Commons has two major roles. Read the comments below. Why is the House of Commons so important? What might happen if the Government could make laws and decisions without having to discuss matters in Parliament?

> The House of Commons plays a major part in introducing new laws. Suggested new laws are debated in the chamber. Once any changes have been made, the MPs then vote whether to accept it or not. If they do accept it, then it goes to the House of Lords to be debated and voted on. Once it has been passed there, it is signed by the monarch and becomes law.

> The House of Commons questions Government policy. MPs can question the Government about anything that affects the UK or about how the Government is running the country. This means that the Government has to be able to explain its actions and plans.

**4.** Greg, Sonia and Maria are all students from the USA who are interested in British politics. You have been asked to give them a guided tour of the House of Commons chamber while Parliament is not in session. Your tour must include information about what the House of Commons is for. It should explain how some of the objects or areas in the chamber are used and it should answer the students' questions. You can write the script or role-play the tour in small groups.

**PLAN**

> How does someone get to be an MP?

> Which party gets to form the Government?

> What is the House of Commons for?

> What is a Prime Minister and who is the Prime Minister at the moment?

> Wouldn't the Government be able to get on better if it didn't have to keep answering questions in the House of Commons about what it's doing?

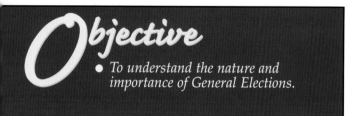

## Election special

1. In a General Election, people vote to decide who will be their Member of Parliament. The party with the most MPs forms the Government. A General Election has to be held within five years of the last one. Why do we have General Elections? Why are they held every five years or less?

2. Jane Pitt wants to stand for election as a Member of Parliament in the General Election. Read the cartoon to find out how Jane gets on.

Jane has been a member of a political party for several years. She has been a councillor and campaigned for her local party. The local party interview Jane and several other people to choose the party candidate.

Jane has been chosen and is now campaigning as a candidate in the constituency. The local party will pay the £500 deposit that candidates have to pay in order to stand for Parliament.

Each political party has published a 'manifesto'. This is a booklet outlining all the promises and plans they will put into action if they are elected. Jane speaks about her party's manifesto at her meetings and she also talks about what she will do for local people.

**KEY WORDS**   General Election   votes   secret ballot   polling booth

On election day, people vote in polling booths by marking an 'X' on a slip of paper next to the name of the person they want to win. This is done in private. Who we vote for can be kept a secret.

Jane received the most votes in her constituency, so she is now the Member of Parliament for that constituency and will take her place in the House of Commons. She must work to represent all her constituents, not just those who voted for her.

**3.** Choose two or three moments from the cartoon and write extracts from Jane's diary describing what she did and how she felt at those times.

**4.** Most candidates belong to a political party, although some stand as independent candidates. If you could form a political party, what would you promise to do if your party won the election? Write a mini manifesto showing what you would try to do. The ideas below might get you started.

**PLAN**

Green Party promises to cut pollution

Conservatives promise to cut tax burden

Labour Party promises more money for schools

Liberal Democrats support rail funding

Plaid Cymru promises to increase number of Welsh-speaking schools

Scottish National Party (SNP) backs university expansion plans

**5.** You will be able to vote in a General Election when you are 18. What responsibility does this right bring? How can you prepare for the responsibility?

# How the Government works

1. The pupils of Whitchurch School have decided to raise money for a skateboard ramp. Each class elected two pupils to lead the fund-raising. There were 66 elected pupils at the first meeting. They soon realised that they needed to get organised, and this is what they came up with:

Whitchurch Fundraisers

**Chairperson**
Alison has been elected as chairperson. She chose a committee of people to help her.

**The Committee**
Dave is treasurer. Monica is secretary. Carly is publicity officer. Imran is events coordinator.

**Event Leaders**
Twenty-seven pupils agreed to organise one fund-raising event each.

**Event Deputies**
Most of the event leaders have a deputy to help them.

**Event Helpers**
Many of the non-elected pupils are helping with particular events.

**CONSIDER**

2. The fund-raising has gone extremely well. Do you think being organised in this way helped? What would have happened if everyone had gone off to do their own thing without anyone coordinating the fund-raising or making decisions?

3. Someone has commented that the way the fund-raisers organised themselves was very similar to how the UK Government is organised. Look at the diagram above. If Alison is the Prime Minister, what is Dave? Who are the Cabinet? Who are the Secretaries of State? Who are the Junior Ministers? Who are the civil servants?

The first woman Prime Minister in the UK was Margaret Thatcher. She was also one of the longest serving Prime Ministers, being in post from 1979 to 1990.

**KEY WORDS** | Minister   Cabinet   Prime Minister   Secretary of State

**The Prime Minister (PM)** – the leader of the party that won the General Election.

**Ministers** – the PM chooses Ministers to run the Government Departments. Nearly all Government Ministers are MPs. Some are from the House of Lords.

**The Cabinet** – some Ministers are chosen by the PM to be in charge of the most important Government Departments. These Ministers, and a few holding other positions, form the Cabinet.

They include the **Chancellor of the Exchequer** – the person responsible for the country's finances.

**Secretaries of State** – each Government Department is headed by a Minister who is responsible for that Department. Their title is 'Secretary of State'. For example the Secretary of State for Education and Employment is head of the Department for Education and Employment (the DfEE). You may hear this person called the 'Education Secretary' for short.

**Junior Ministers** – departments also have Junior Ministers to help with the work.

**Civil Service** – this is the organisation that carries out the work of the Government but it is not part of the Government itself. Civil servants are not elected and they are not MPs. They work for the Ministers in the Government Departments.

**4.** Is your school organisation similar to the UK Government? Who is the Prime Minister? Who is in the Cabinet? What role do the Heads of Year or Heads of Department play?

**5.** Imagine you are the Prime Minister. You have been invited on to a children's television programme to answer children's questions about the Government. Some of the questions you are asked are given below. Role-play or write the script for the programme.

**ROLE–PLAY**

How did you get to be Prime Minister?

How is the Government organised?

What is the Cabinet and why is it important?

Why does the Government need so many secretaries?

Does the Cabinet vote on issues?

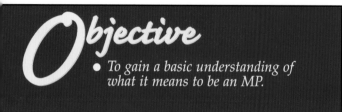

*Objective*
● To gain a basic understanding of what it means to be an MP.

# The work of an MP

**CONSIDER**

1. Jane Pitt is an MP. What does 'MP' stand for and how does someone get to be an MP?

2. The cartoon below shows Jane at work. Make a list of the activities Jane is involved in as an MP.

Jane has given up her job as a lecturer to work as an MP. MPs are paid around £48 000, plus expenses, per year. Some MPs continue to do other paid work but they have to declare who they work for (and what they earn).

Jane spends most mornings in her office. She reads reports and other information and replies to letters from her constituents.

*Would the Prime Minister please tell me whether or not any of the new business grants will be made available to the textile industry?*

Jane spends some of her time listening and contributing to debates in the House of Commons Chamber. These can go on until 10.30pm or later. Occasionally, she will ask a question during Prime Minister's question time on behalf of her constituents.

The House of Commons sits for about 170 days a year and is closed for several months over the summer.

**KEY WORDS** | Member of Parliament   elected   constituents   constituency

*... and we need to discuss the new rail transport proposals.*

Jane is a member of several committees and often meets with them to discuss matters and make proposals.

Jane returns to her constituency every weekend and holds a 'surgery' every second Monday morning so that constituents can discuss their concerns with her. When Parliament is closed over the summer, Jane takes a two week holiday and spends the rest of the time working in her constituency.

**RESEARCH**

**3.** Using the information from the cartoon and any other resources you can find, produce a fact file with the title 'The job of an MP'. You could include how someone becomes an MP, what the job involves, and the skills and qualities they need to do it well.

**4.** MPs represent their constituents, so they need to know their views. Find out the name of your local MP and write a letter to him or her giving your views on something that matters to you. As a class, decide which letters to send.

**CONSIDER**

**5.** Do you think MPs should be allowed to earn money from other work when they are being paid as MPs? List the pros (advantages) and cons (disadvantages) of this:
   **a.** from the point of view of the MP
   **b.** from the point of view of Parliament
   **c.** from the point of view of a voter in the constituency.

# Forms of government

**BRAINSTORM**

**1.** Your class has been chosen to spend a year on a remote island. Many decisions will have to be made on the island. Brainstorm all the ways decisions could be made. Remember to include ideas you wouldn't like as well as those you think would work.

**DISCUSS**

**2.** Working in groups of about four, discuss the ideas and decide which system you think will work best. Share your ideas as a class. Each group should give reasons for their decision.

**3.** Decisions within countries can also be made in a number of ways. Read the comments below. What might be the good things and the bad things about living in each country?

Some years ago, a group of army generals took over the leadership of our country. There had been a lot of fighting and they claimed that they needed to bring order. Most of the fighting has stopped, but anyone who disagrees with the Government is imprisoned or worse. The Government doesn't seem interested in education or health for ordinary people but what can we do?

We do not have elections. We are ruled by a royal family. The King is head of the Government and most of the Ministers are members of the same family. It is a traditional way of government.

**FACT TO THINK ABOUT ... FACT TO THINK ABOUT ... FACT TO THINK ABOUT ...**

In some countries, the Government owns the newspapers and the radio and television companies. This means they can control much of what people know.

**KEY WORDS**    democracy   government   elected   leader   president

> We do have elections, but there is only one party to vote for. There are great differences between rich people and poor people in this country. Many of the top people in the ruling party enjoy wonderful lifestyles, most of the ordinary people do not.

> Our country is led by an elected President but he doesn't have complete power. He has to work within the law, and new laws can only be passed if they are voted in by Congress. The politicians in Congress have all been elected. Unfortunately, many people don't believe that the politicians care for them. Only half the population bother to vote.

**4.** Write a statement similar to the ones above describing how your country is governed.

**5.** Chan lives in a country where people have very little say about how the country is run. Read his comment, then write a letter to Chan answering his questions. You may find the following words useful:

> election   voting   campaign   petition   letter writing

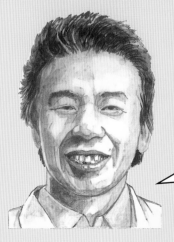

> In my country, the Government control everything and people are not allowed to protest. I have heard that, in a democracy, people have many ways of making the Government take notice of their opinions. How do people do this? How can people affect the way the country is run?

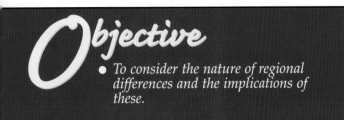

# Objective

- To consider the nature of regional differences and the implications of these.

# Regional differences

1. The young people below have all moved to a different region from the one they were born in. What differences, if any, do you think they would each have found when they moved?

| | | | |
|---|---|---|---|
| Akim moved from Glasgow to Exeter. | Gerri moved from Norwich to Manchester. | Daniel moved from London to the Yorkshire Dales. | Wesley moved from Swansea to Birmingham. |

2. Many people have ideas about what people from different parts of the country are like. How far do you think the comments on page 63 are true? Where do ideas like this come from? Are they harmless or dangerous?

In a recent survey, it was found that people with north-eastern accents were less likely to find well-paid jobs in London than those with southern accents.

**KEY WORDS**     region    accent    dialect    tradition    culture

> I can always tell where someone comes from by what they're like. Geordies and Scousers, they're friendly. Glasgow blokes – they drink loads and you don't want to pick a fight with them 'cos they can turn nasty. Southerners are really stuck up and posh – apart from Cockneys – they're a good laugh. The lot down in the West Country are all slow, takes them ages to do anything. Same's true of Norfolk folk – they'll tell you anything you want to know about a tractor but don't ask 'em about computers – they won't have a clue.

**3.** Many regions have a culture and traditions that they work hard to keep alive. In Derbyshire, there is a tradition going back to the seventeenth century of making 'well dressings'. A well dressing is a picture made out of thousands of individual flower petals, grains of rice, leaves, moss or any other natural materials, which are stuck on to a clay backing to create a picture. Read the comment below:

> The tradition is thought to derive originally from the pagan practice of giving thanks for water. The custom was revived in Derbyshire in the seventeenth century and has been going ever since. Most well dressings are made in spring. They are often, but not always, on a religious theme. They take many hours and many people to make, and they fade in about five days! It seems a lot of hard work but we are very proud of them and villages compete to create the best dressing.

**4.** What benefits might the tradition of well dressing have for Derbyshire and its people? Do you think traditions like this are worth keeping alive?

**5.** Design a well dressing or poster of your own region, showing all the things that are special about it.

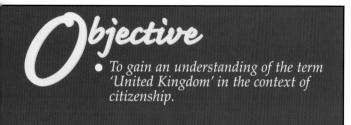
# Being a part of the UK

**BRAINSTORM**

1. What does the word 'United' mean? What does the word 'Kingdom' mean? Why do we call this place where we live the 'United Kingdom'?

2. How much do you know about the United Kingdom?
   a. Which countries make up the United Kingdom?
   b. What is the approximate population of the UK? **i)** 10 million **ii)** 35 million or **iii)** 60 million.
   c. What is the area of the UK? **i)** 244 755 square kilometres **ii)** 580 335 square kilometres or **iii)** 10 002 300 square kilometres.
   d. What does the Union flag look like and where does its design come from?

3. The United Kingdom hasn't always been united. Read the information below to find out how we got to where we are today.

In 1282, King Edward I of England gained a military conquest over Wales. Wales became joined to England formally in 1536 and 1543 under King Henry VIII.

In 1603, James VI of Scotland succeeded to the English throne and became James I of England and Wales. A common Parliament, governing all three countries, was established in 1707.

**FACT TO THINK ABOUT ... FACT TO THINK ABOUT ... FACT TO THINK ABOUT ...**

The British Isles became separated from the mainland of Europe about 12 000 years ago when the sea levels rose after the last ice age.

**KEY WORDS**  United Kingdom  citizenship  Union flag

In 1801, Ireland was united with the rest of the British Isles to form The United Kingdom of Great Britain and Ireland. In 1922, Southern Ireland became independent and became the Republic of Ireland. Northern Ireland remained a part of the UK.

In 1997, the people of Scotland and Wales voted in favour of 'devolution', which led to the setting up of the Scottish Parliament and the Welsh Assembly. The people of Northern Ireland voted in favour of devolution in 1998 and the Northern Ireland Assembly was formed as a result of this and as part of the peace process. The Government in London shares some of its powers with the Scottish Parliament, the Welsh Assembly and the Northern Ireland Assembly.

**CONSIDER**

4. Terry Waite once said, "It is only when you know how to be a citizen of your own country that you can learn how to be a citizen of the world." In groups, make a list of what it means to be a citizen of the UK. How is being a citizen of the UK different from being a citizen of another country?

5. Use the information on this page and your own ideas to design a quiz for 11-year-old pupils about the United Kingdom and being a citizen of the United Kingdom.

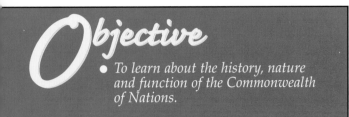

*Objective*
- To learn about the history, nature and function of the Commonwealth of Nations.

# The Commonwealth of Nations

**CONSIDER**

1. The Commonwealth of Nations is a group of 54 countries that have agreed to work together to improve the lives of people living in their countries. Most of the countries once had strong links with the UK because they were once British colonies, which means that they were ruled by Britain. When they became independent, they chose to keep some links with the UK and, since then, some other countries have also joined.

   Think about the words 'common wealth'. What do you think they mean? (Remember – being wealthy may mean more than having money.)

2. The Commonwealth does not have any laws and it cannot make countries behave in a particular way. It is simply an agreement that governments and people will share ideas, look for solutions to problems and work together. Some of the links created by the Commonwealth are shown below. How could each one improve the lives of people living in the Commonwealth?

**A.** Prime Ministers and Presidents of Commonwealth countries meet every two years to discuss issues such as improving education, supporting immunisation campaigns, preventing the spread of HIV and AIDS or ways to combat prejudice. These meetings are called 'Heads of Government meetings' or HOGMs.

**B.** Many professions belong to Commonwealth groups so that they can share ideas. For example, there is a Commonwealth Dental Association, which aims to improve dental care throughout Commonwealth countries.

**C.** The Commonwealth Games are held every four years. This is a major international sporting event.

Over 1.6 billion people live in Commonwealth countries – that's over a quarter of the world's population.

**KEY WORDS**    Commonwealth    racial discrimination    multi-faith

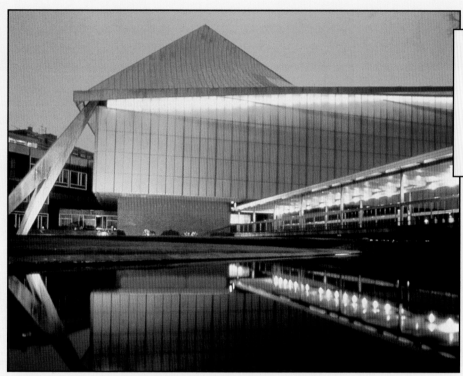

**D.** The Commonwealth Institute in London holds festivals, displays and events celebrating the lives of people around the Commonwealth.

**3.** Imagine the next Heads of Government meeting invited young people to share in their discussions about how the Commonwealth countries could help each other. Make a list of the points you would raise at that meeting. For each point you give, you should provide reasons for including it.

**4.** There are Commonwealth countries in every continent. The Commonwealth includes some of the richest and some of the poorest countries, some of the biggest and some of the smallest. Every year, a multi-faith service is held in Westminster Abbey to celebrate the Commonwealth. Write a prayer or poem that could be used in the service.

**5.** When Heads of Government meet, they often do so in their regions (Europe, Asia and so on) and in 'common-interest' groups (rich countries, poor countries, oil producers and so on). How is the Commonwealth different? How might this help both rich and poor countries?

**BRAINSTORM**

*What good are links with the Commonwealth? I just like to sit down in the evening with a cup of tea and a nice Indian takeaway. Tonight I'll talk to the kids about their new teacher – she's from Australia, over here for two years.*

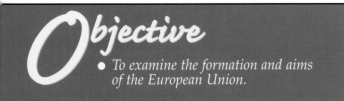

# What is the European Union?

1. European history is full of accounts of conflict and wars. In the last century, the First and Second World Wars killed millions of people and wrecked the lives of millions more. Since the Second World War, many people saw the advantages of a more united Europe. On 1 January 1958, the 'European Economic Community' (as the EU was first known) came into existence.

The original six countries were: France, West Germany, Italy, Belgium, the Netherlands and Luxembourg.

**IMAGINE**

Imagine you lived in one of the founding countries. What would you want from membership of the EU? Draw up a list of what you would want to achieve from membership.

**1951**
Frenchman Jean Monnet believed that countries with close trading links were less likely to make war against each other. At his suggestion, France, West Germany, Belgium, Italy, Luxembourg and the Netherlands all agreed to link their coal and steel industries under one organisation called the European Coal and Steel Community. This linked the countries together, making it necessary for them to work together.

**1957**
The six countries created the European Economic Community, which made other trade between the six countries easier and cheaper.

**1963 onwards**
The six countries offered financial help to developing countries in Africa. In return, those African countries agreed to trade with the six European countries. Similar agreements were set up with other areas. Other European countries began to feel they might be losing out on trade opportunities.

**1970s onwards**
Nine other countries, including the UK, joined the original six. Other agreements were signed.

**1973**
1 January – Britain became a member of the EU.

**1979**
A European Parliament was set up with elected representatives from each member country.

**1993**
The Treaty of European Union was signed, opening up the way for a single European currency and removing the last of the regulations that prevented easy trade between member countries. The group became known as the European Union. Other countries have applied to join.

## FACTS TO THINK ABOUT ... FACTS TO THINK ABOUT ... FACTS TO THINK ABOUT

The European Union flag has 12 stars on it. At one time there were 12 member states, but the significance goes back to a European Christian tradition, where the Virgin Mary originally had 12 stars in her halo, signifying the 12 apostles. This number also represents the 12 signs of the zodiac and the 12 months of the Western year.

**KEY WORDS**    Europe   European Union   economic   political

The European Union now deals with more than just issues of trade. The European Parliament can make rulings that member countries have to abide by on issues like immigration, the police, the law and systems of justice and defence against non-European countries.

**2.** Look at the two statements below. Which one do you agree with most? Why? Write a statement that sums up your beliefs about being a part of Europe.

**CONSIDER**

*We are already Europeans. Being part of the Union makes it easier for people to travel and work in other EU countries. It opens up opportunities for people.*

*If we get tied to Europe we will lose our identity as a nation. We want to be British, with a British culture. It's not right that people from other countries should make laws that affect us.*

**3.** Before a country can join the EU it must give guarantees of democracy, human rights and the protection of minority peoples. Is this fair? Why is it felt to be important?

**4.** One of the aims of the EU is to improve the living and working conditions of Europe's citizens. Brainstorm groups of people who may suffer from poor living or working conditions. What could be done to improve their lives? Do you think being a part of the EU will help them?

**BRAINSTORM**

**O**bjective

● To examine how being a member of the European Union can affect individuals.

# An individual in Europe

**1.** The United Kingdom joined the European Community in 1973. In 1975, people were asked to vote in a referendum to see if public opinion supported the decision to join; the public voted 2:1 in favour of 'staying in Europe'. Despite this, many people still worry that being part of the European Union will mean that the United Kingdom will be controlled by Europe. The two news articles below show different views about the EU. Begin by reading the articles.

---

**THE DAILY NEWS**                                   *Tuesday 18th December 2001*

# EU Roadshow a huge success

Residents of Clacton were surprised to see a caravan flying the EU flag sitting in the main street on Saturday, but many were curious enough to look inside. What they found was a display of information about the benefits of belonging to the EU. Organisers were delighted with the amount of people visiting. Roadshow manager Pam Cape said, "The aim of the roadshow is to get people talking about the EU and combat some of the ridiculous myths that are around. We don't necessarily want to convert everyone to our way of thinking – although that would be nice – but if everyone who leaves carried away just one piece of information then that would be progress." Here's a selection of some of the information visitors might have picked up.

'Being part of a single currency would have enormous benefits. It would be a very stable currency because things that might affect one country would be "ironed out" by conditions in other countries.'

'The EU has 370.4 million citizens. That's a huge market, and people are bound to prefer trading with a single currency rather than having to convert. The combined countries of the EU also account for over 30 per cent of the world's trade –

we would be crazy not to be a part of it.'

'We've already benefitted. Britain wouldn't be half so advanced in terms of its anti-discrimination policies if it wasn't for pressure from the EU. No one really took things like sexual discrimination and rights for disabled people seriously until the European Court of Justice took up some of the cases.'

'We can't afford to be isolated. The world is a smaller place now, thanks to fast travel and the Internet, so anything that helps us get on with our neighbours has got to be a good thing.'

## FACT TO THINK ABOUT ... FACT TO THINK ABOUT ... FACT TO THINK ABOUT ...

Norway has twice successfully applied for membership of the EU, and twice the population has rejected it by referendum.

**KEY WORDS**    regulation    pro-Europe    anti-Europe    EU directive

---

THE CLARION                                                    *Friday 1st February 2002*

# Don't mess with my scales!

Market trader Tony Greer was on the Euro warpath yesterday when officials removed his set of weights used for measuring out fruit and veg. European directives state that loose produce should be sold in metric measurements but Tony still uses the same pounds and ounces weights that his father used before him. When asked to comment, Mr Greer, aged 47 said, "It's ridiculous. My customers don't want these foreign measurements; they want what they know. Pounds and ounces have been good enough for hundreds of years, I don't see why we should let a decision made hundreds of miles away affect us."
Supporters of the anti-Europe campaign agreed with Mr Greer's comments. One anti-Europe supporter said, "For one thing, the legislations coming in from Europe are so longwinded and complicated that you need a degree in law to understand them. I saw a directive the other day that actually stated that bent cucumbers could not be sold alongside straight ones. Where will it end?" Other anti-Europeans have more fundamental objections to the UK's role in Europe. Lecturer Chris Naptal said, "the trouble with the EU is that EU laws can't take account of local conditions. What's right for one country may not apply to another. We are not all the same." Meanwhile, Mr Greer has found a new way to sell his produce: "I use tins of baked beans now – a tin of beans and a small potato weighs about a pound. I daresay they'll take my beans now."

---

**2.** List the benefits of being in the EU according to the articles. List the disadvantages of being in the EU according to the articles.

**3.** Write or role-play a conversation between one person who believes the UK should be a part of the EU and another person who believes the UK should not.

**ROLE–PLAY**

**4.** Reg Walker, a 46-year-old shopkeeper is anti-European. Read his comment.

> We fought the war to stay British. If we give in to all this European rubbish then we will lose all the things that make Britain British.

**5.** Brainstorm things that could be said to make Britain 'British'. Which of these, if any, would be lost if Britain stays a part of the European Union? Do you agree with Reg or not?

# The World Health Organisation

**CONSIDER**

1. WHO stands for the World Health Organisation. It is an agency of the United Nations and was founded in 1946. WHO aims to:
   ● give worldwide guidance in the field of health
   ● work with governments to improve national health programmes
   ● develop and help to spread health technology, information and standards.

   The statement below is the WHO definition of health. Why do they define health in these terms? According to the WHO definition, would somebody who was lonely and afraid all the time be healthy, even if they were not ill? Who else would not be healthy according to the WHO definition?

> Health is a state of complete physical, mental and social well-being and not merely the absence of disease or infirmity.

2. One of the roles of WHO is to carry out research and provide health information to help countries and organisations make decisions about health care. WHO have developed the DALE chart. Read about DALE below, then use the chart to answer the questions on page 73.

> WHO recognises that quality of life is as important as length of life, and they have developed a calculation to work out the number of healthy years a person might be expected to have. This is called the Disability Adjusted Life Expectancy (DALE).

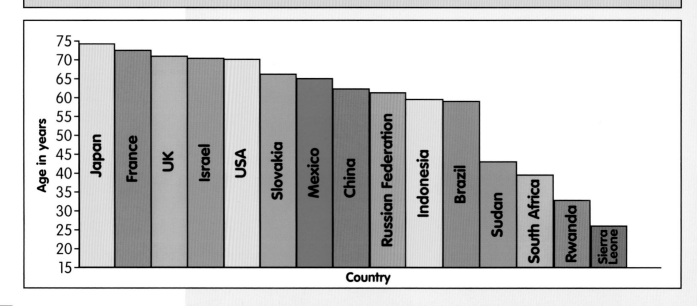

FACT TO THINK ABOUT ... FACT TO THINK ABOUT ... FACT TO THINK ABOUT ...

WHO has saved seven million children from river blindness over the years.

| **KEY WORDS** | life expectancy   healthy life   disease   poverty |
|---|---|

**a.** Which continent has the lowest DALE?

**b.** What is the difference in years between the country with the highest DALE and the country with the lowest DALE?

**c.** Of the 191 countries on the full DALE chart, the life expectancy in 24 countries equals or exceeds 70 years, and in over half the countries exceeds 60 years, but 32 countries have a DALE below 40 years. What problems would you expect to find in countries with the lowest DALE?

**d.** What conclusions can you draw from this chart?

**e.** How could a chart like this help countries and the WHO in planning medical services, research and funding?

**3.** The USA has a lower DALE than many other developed countries. Imagine you are a WHO official. Put together a report exploring the reasons why the USA has a lower DALE rating than others, suggesting a programme for improving disability adjusted life expectancy. The pictures below may give you some ideas.

**PLAN**

Some groups, such as Native Americans and inner city poor, have extremely poor health.

The HIV epidemic affects many young people.

High rates of lung cancer.

High rates of heart disease.

High rates of violence, especially murders, compared with other industrial countries.

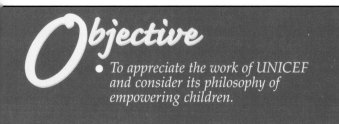

**Objective**
● To appreciate the work of UNICEF and consider its philosophy of empowering children.

# Teaching tomorrow's adults

**1.** The United Nations is an international organisation that aims to promote world peace and improve people's lives. UNICEF is the United Nations Children's Fund. UNICEF believes that children should be protected, but it also believes that children are the key to improving the world for the future. Read the stories below, which show some of the UNICEF projects aimed at empowering children.

Many people in my country are killed or disabled by landmines left here from conflicts. Children are victims because they often tend animals or play in the fields. UNICEF has trained me and other 12 to 14-year-olds to help teach children about the danger of landmines. I travel around the countryside leading workshops. I may be speaking to up to 40 children aged six to fourteen to tell them about the dangers, teach them to recognise the minefield signs and show them what to look out for. We talk about where mines might be found and what to do if they see one or if someone is injured. They listen because they see I am like them. I hope I have saved some lives.

Education is important but school hours are very short in Peru. Project '2x1' enables older children like me to help younger children with their education. I meet with two eight-year-old boys at weekends and evenings to help them with reading, writing and maths. The project workers showed me what to do, and they give me ideas as well as some books and paper. The project is called '2x1' because one activity helps two people. The younger children are learning education, but it also helps me because I am now more confident, I care about other people and I know that I can make a difference to Peru. Before I joined this project, I was in a street gang. I would be in big trouble by now if it wasn't for this project.

**FACT TO THINK ABOUT ... FACT TO THINK ABOUT ... FACT TO THINK ABOUT ...**

A poll of four million children across Latin America found that they rated the right to an education as the most important right of a child.

**KEY WORDS**    empowering    benefits    refugee    landmine

My country has been badly affected by war and there are many refugees like me. When I first came to this camp I had nothing to do but now I have been trained as a child carer. Every morning, I go to the children's centre, where children aged three to six are brought to play and learn. I help them draw, play, sing songs and other things. It is the happiest place in the camp. Many girls my age have been trained for this job. We learned about how children learn, how to look after them, how to keep them healthy and how to deal with problems. I'd like to train as a teacher one day.

**2.** In groups, choose one of the above projects and talk about:
  – how the project helps the younger children
  – how the project helps the older children
  – how the project will help the country as a whole as the children grow up.

**DISCUSS**

**3.** Imagine you have been given some money to set up a project in your area where young people aged 12 to 14 help younger children in some way. Put together an outline for a project including:
  – the aim of the project
  – what will happen
  – what resources you will need
  – what training will be needed.

**PLAN**

**4.** Read the statement below. Why do you think UNICEF chooses to use children rather than adults in these projects? Do you think UNICEF is right?

**CONSIDER**

UNICEF shouldn't waste money training older children to work with younger children. For one thing, adults would do a better job than the children, and for another thing, the older children shouldn't be expected to take serious responsibilities like these at such a young age.

# Drug information

| Drug | Information | Effects | Risks |
|------|-------------|---------|-------|
| **Cannabis** | Can be dried leaves or in a solid 'resin'. Is usually smoked with tobacco but can be eaten. | Makes users relaxed and talkative. The user may become especially aware of colours, taste and music. | Can affect short-term memory and ability to concentrate, so it would be difficult to drive. Users can feel afraid or anxious. If smoked with tobacco, carries usual risks of smoking, including lung cancer. Can be difficult to give up. |
| **Cocaine** | A white powder that can be snorted up the nose. Some users inject it. | Creates a powerful buzz, making users feel alert and confident for about 30 minutes. | Users often crave for more. Can cause heart problems and chest pain. Large or frequent use can cause convulsions ('fits'), feelings of restlessness, confusion and fear. Snorting can damage inside of nose. Addictive. Users have died of overdoses. |
| **Ecstasy** | Usually taken as small tablets, sometimes with a picture or an 'E' on them. | Users feel alert and energetic. Sounds, colours and emotions may feel more intense. Effects can last from three to six hours. | Can cause tightening of the jaw, nausea, sweating and increase in heart rate. Use has been linked to kidney and liver problems. Users may feel tired and depressed for days after use. There have been over 70 ecstasy-related deaths in the UK. |

# Drug information

| Drug | Information | Effects | Risks |
|------|-------------|---------|-------|
| **Heroin** | A white powder when pure. Street heroin is usually mixed with other substances and can be brownish-white. It is snorted, smoked or injected. | Small doses can lead to feelings of warmth and well-being, higher doses can make the user feel drowsy and relaxed. | Very addictive. Very difficult to give up. User needs more and more to get the same 'fix', and getting the next fix can take over their lives completely. Users often end up needing the drug just to feel nearly normal. Can cause dizziness and vomiting. An overdose can kill. |
| **LSD** | Usually comes as tiny squares of paper with a picture on one side. | Users experience a 'trip' or hallucination, which means seeing, hearing or feeling things that are not there. Effects depend on the user's mood and surroundings. Sense of movement and time may speed up or slow down. Objects, sound or colour may become distorted. Trips can last up to 12 hours. | Users cannot predict whether the trip will be 'good' or 'bad'. A bad trip may be terrifying and, during the trip, users may not be aware that the drug is responsible and so believe that what they are experiencing is real. Danger of accidents during hallucinations. Users may feel frightened and out of control for a long time afterwards. 'Flashbacks' may occur, where the user relives parts of a trip, days, weeks or even years afterwards. LSD can make problems or worries worse. |
| **Speed** | Grey or white powder, or sometimes tablets. Can be snorted, swallowed, injected or smoked. | A stimulant. Quickens heart rate and breathing. Users may feel confident, ultra-alert and energetic. | Users may feel tired and depressed for one or two days after use. Frequent, high doses may cause panic and hallucinations. Long-term users may become dependent on it and need to use more and more to get the same effects. Long-term use can damage the heart. Speed can lead to mental illness such as psychosis. Overdose can be fatal. Speed is often mixed with other substances. |

# Answers

## KEEPING SAFE – CONTRACEPTION

1  a. Femidom
   b. spermicidal foam
   c. diaphragm
   d. cervical cap
   e. condom
   f. sponge
   g. contraceptive pill
   h. IUD
   i. test for hormone levels (natual method)
   j. morning after pill

## SEXUALLY TRANSMITTED INFECTIONS

2  a. They are all STIs except the Fibonacci series which is a mathematical concept.

   b  i. False. Many people with STIs have no symptoms for a very long time.

      ii. False. Many people with STIs have no symptoms. Needing to urinate frequently may be a sign of an STI or other medical problem, or may simply be the result of having had a large amount to drink. Someone who finds they constantly need the toilet frequently should consult a doctor just in case.

      iii. True. Some people with STIs have no symptoms and sometimes symptoms may go away although the infection is still present. All of the symptoms described could be caused by other medical problems as well.

      iv. False. If either partner has had one or more previous partners then either one may already have unknowingly contracted an STI.

      v. False. Although this is true of many STIs, some, such as genital warts or HIV, have no permanent cure (although the symptoms may be controlled).

   c. Anyone suspecting they may have an STI should see a doctor. This could be their own GP but they could also go to a family planning clinic or a GUM clinic. GUM stands for genito-urinary medicine and these clinics (occasionally still known as special clinics) can be found in the phone book or by phoning the local hospital. They are part of the NHS and will see patients in complete confidence. It is best to phone or call in to make an appointment but if the problem is urgent someone will usually see the patient straight away.

3. The only character safe from STIs is the virgin (assuming he doesn't inject drugs). The characters who have reduced their risk of contracting STIs are the woman who always uses a condom and the man with only one partner. The drug-user and woman who has many partners have a higher risk of contracting STIs.

## HIV AND AIDS – WHAT'S THE DIFFERENCE?

2  a. False. Someone can be HIV positive for years before becoming ill.

   b. True. It is the virus (HIV) that is passed on. AIDS describes the symptoms that occur as a result of the HIV.

   c. True.

   d. True.

   e. True.

   f. False. HIV positive means someone has the virus. HIV negative means that they did not have the virus at the time the test was taken. Someone who has been tested as HIV negative may have contracted the virus after the test was carried out.

## LEARNING TO RELAX

1. Physical responses to stress include: increased heart rate, increased blood pressure, increased rate of breathing, increased muscle tension and sweating. These are caused by an increase in particular hormones, which is thought to be an evolved response enabling the person under stress to fight or run away. Signs of relaxation include: lowered blood pressure, slower breathing and reduced muscle tension.

# Answers

## EMERGENCY AID

1. Fainting may be a reaction to pain, fright or an emotional upset. It could be caused by exhaustion or lack of food. Fainting is common after long periods of inactivity, such as standing still, especially in a warm place. Fainting could be a symptom of a medical disorder and someone who faints more than once in a short period of time, or who faints for no apparent reason, should see a doctor.

   Causes of unconsciousness include: head injury, lack of oxygen (which may be caused by choking, suffocation, smoke or poisonous fumes), a heart attack, stroke, epilepsy, diabetes or poisoning (including abuse of alcohol, solvents or drugs).

2. Suggested guidelines for dealing with a person who has fainted:
   - Check to see whether the person is wearing a bracelet or necklace warning of a medical condition and, if they are, check what it says.
   - Lay the casualty down, support the legs in a raised position.
   - Make sure there is nothing restricting breathing and open a window or door, particularly if it is hot.
   - Stop people from crowding around.
   - If the person does not begin to recover quickly, get someone to call an ambulance.
   - As they recover, help them to sit up gently and slowly. Don't rush to get them into a chair or standing position.
   - Reassure them that they are going to be fine.

3. The recovery position is lying down so the patient cannot fall and the blood is able to circulate more easily. The chest is open, making breathing easier, the head is tilted so that the person's tongue will fall forward, and not back into the throat where it could choke the patient. If the patient is sick, the vomit can run away easily, which will prevent the patient from choking. A patient who is not breathing should not be put in the recovery position and should be given artificial respiration immediately.

## KNOWING THE LAW

3. Class A drugs include cocaine, crack, ecstasy, heroin, LSD, speed prepared for injection and prepared magic mushrooms. Class B drugs include cannabis and speed. Class C drugs include steroids, tranquillisers and temazepam obtained without a doctor's prescription.

4. a. They have not broken the law by picking the mushrooms, but if they make them into a drink they will have broken the law and be in possession of a class A drug. In practice, maximum prosecutions are not usually given for magic mushrooms.
   b. They have committed an offence. If this was a first offence they would be likely to receive a caution.
   c. Pete is breaking the law by trying to buy ecstasy. Under the circumstances, Maria would probably be cautioned. If Pete was using Maria regularly to buy drugs he could face other charges.
   d. Gareth has broken the law. His mother would be breaking the law if she knowingly let him smoke cannabis in her house.

## RECOGNISING DRUGS

1. a. Cannabis     iii
   b. LSD     vi
   c. Amphetamines     i
   d. Cocaine     ii
   e. Heroin     iv
   f. Ecstasy     v

## CONSUMER POWER

2. a. 'Fully Air-cushioned' is not a precise description, but even so, the term implies that the trainers have air cushioning in more than just one place, so the goods are *not as described*.
   b. The computer game was *not fit for the purpose* it was sold for.
   c. The top was only advertised as 'cotton rich' not '100% cotton', so the shop has not broken any laws. Many shops, however, have a policy of refunding the money or giving a credit note if the goods are returned quickly, undamaged and with a receipt.
   d. The shoes were *not of satisfactory quality*. Even if the shoes had been advertised as 'fashion shoes', shoes are meant to be worn, and breaking within a week is unreasonable.

# Answers

## LOCAL GOVERNMENT

1. Each school differs and some or all of the decisions would probably have been discussed by a number of people, but the most likely people to have made each decision are:
a and f – class teacher
c and d – headteacher
b and e – governors.

## INSIDE THE HOUSE OF COMMONS

1.

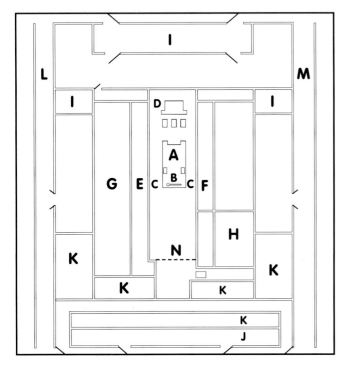

## BEING A PART OF THE UK

2 **a.** England, Wales, Scotland and Northern Ireland

**b.** iii

**c.** i

**d.** The Union flag embodies the emblems of the three kingdoms which make up the UK, namely:

- St George is the patron saint of England. His flag, a red cross on a white background, was the emblem of England and Wales when James I, VI of Scotland, came to the throne.

- St Andrew is the patron saint of Scotland. His flag, a diagonal white cross on a blue background, was combined with the St George cross after Scotland was united with England and Wales.

- St Patrick is the patron saint of Ireland. His flag, a diagonal red cross on a white background, was combined with the previous Union flag when Ireland became part of the UK.

The Welsh emblem of a dragon is not represented, which may seem unfair. Historically, this is because the St George cross had been used to represent both England and Wales for a long time before the Scottish flag was added.

## THE WORLD HEALTH ORGANISATION

2 **d.** Africa is the continent with the lowest DALE, due to many aspects, including: war, poverty, lack of food, lack of medical care and comparatively high rates of AIDS. The difference between the countries with the highest and lowest DALE (Japan and Sierra Leone) is 48.6 years.